ACHIEVING CHANGE

Achieving Change

a systematic approach

Tom Lupton
and
Ian Tanner

Gower

Published by
Gower Publishing Company Limited,
Gower House,
Croft Road,
Aldershot,
Hants GU11 3HR,
England

Gower Publishing Company,
Old Post Road,
Brookfield,
Vermont 05036,
USA

British Library Cataloguing in Publication Data

Lupton, Tom
   Achieving change: a systematic approach.
   1. Organizational change
   I. Title   II. Tanner, Ian
   658.4'06   HD58.8

ISBN 0–566–02526–4

Typeset in Great Britain by
Guildford Graphics Limited, Petworth, West Sussex.
Printed in Great Britain at the University Press, Cambridge

Contents

Introduction		vii
1	Making a start	1
2	Dealing with blockages	31
3	Planning for action	45
4	Learning from experience	73
5	Choosing objectives	81

Introduction

This book was written mainly with managers and students of management in mind. As consultants and action-researchers, and in our work with managers attending courses at the Manchester Business School, we have devised and developed a practical method for organisational improvement which makes planning and making changes more effective. The method has been tested and refined in use. Our present purpose is to explain and to illustrate the method to a wider audience and to show the benefits it can bring.

This is not a book about theory; yet like all practical matters our method has a basis in theory. We believe that continuous learning is much enhanced if the theory on which practice is based is made plain and if that theory is modified by the experience of practice. We have relied very much on modern organisation theory and although our main purpose is to show the reader how to use our method, we shall refer to that theory whenever it seems appropriate. It is certainly not our intention, however, to let the theory get in the way. Yet it is our hope and expectation that our readers will be interested in the theory and will not regard our method as just another package to be tried without truly being understood.

Those of our readers who are engineers may see some similarities in our method and presentation to the procedures of engineering design. Like the designer we certainly go from logical step to logical step with detailed instructions on how to proceed, leaving room for modification to meet the specific design objective and the circumstances of the case. However, the similarities end there.

Human enterprises are only partly the outcome of deliberate design. Planning and making changes in them is rarely trouble free. Work organisations are unlike the devices that engineers cleverly put together from the lifeless materials at their disposal. The human beings who are assembled to contribute their various talents to the purposes of enterprises are far from lifeless. Indeed, the difficulties managers face when contemplating or making changes arise from the fact that enterprises want solutions to problems simply stated. Our position is that although practical solutions must always be simple for the reason that everything cannot be done at once such solutions can go very wrong in application if the problem has been over-simply, and therefore misleadingly, stated. It is common in our experience for painful symptoms to be treated as basic causes.

For example, when difficulties arise for managers in the administration of payment systems it is easy to conclude that the problem to be solved lies in the design or administration of the payment system. That conclusion could well be correct, but it could equally be that the difficulties reported with the payment system are symptoms of a malfunctioning of the relationship between the pay system and the system of work-flow planning and administration. The best solution might be to improve the work-flow to fit the existing pay system design. It is difficult to see how one could arrive at a decision about a new design without an examination of the connections between that design and other elements of the production system. Not only work-flow administration, but technology, product variety, and so on. To arrive at a 'simple' solution which will be right in the sense of improving the functioning of the whole organisation, requires a deeper diagnosis which explores the sometimes very complex relationships between a large number of system elements, and between them and elements in the organisation's environment taking into account their inter-dependencies also.

We appreciate the point that has often been made to us that experienced managers do in fact work intuitively with complex multi-variate models of their own organisations or the parts of them that they manage. They decide quickly on fairly simple courses of action with improvement in mind based on their intuitive diagnoses and these courses of action do often lead to the predicted improvements. To the extent that the managers we observe succeed in what they set out to do we are tempted to imitate their decisions and actions rather than to explore and make explicit their intuitive diagnostic frameworks. We ask only 'what do successful managers do, so that we can imitate them?' and neglect to ask 'what is the reasoning behind the intuitive, successful planning of change, and the organisational processes of acceptance and smooth implementation?'. It is the second question that has interested us most and has led us to our present approaches to the process of making changes. To follow only what successful managers do and not to explore the reasoning is hazardous because circumstances differ so much.

The planning of change

Our method is designed to combine and integrate two processes that are usually only loosely connected.

The first is the rational-thinking process which can be illustrated by the following sequence.

1   The manager encounters a difficulty, usually in the form of information that something is happening within the area of his jurisdiction which was not what he wanted to or expected to happen. We can describe that as 'the pain'.

2   The manager *thinks* 'what kind of problem do I have to solve in order to overcome the difficulty?' and asks 'is the pain the result of personal incompetence, technical design, organisation structure, motivation, administrative procedure, a combination of these or what?'

3   The manager now has to decide what kind of information he should look for as evidence of the detailed nature of the problem, such as documents or

personal testimonies, and of whom to ask what kinds of questions.

4   The manager, having examined the evidence, *reasons* that such and such a course of action will solve the problem or contribute to its solution and hence 'ease the pain'.

5   The manager sets the objective towards which the course of action is to be directed and orders, instructs, persuades or negotiates with others, to have these courses of action pursued.

6   The manager will in some way discover whether the course of action he prescribed and ordered did in fact have the outcome that his reasoning led him to expect. He usually learns quickly if it did not when the difficulty persists, in which case he has to go through all the steps again. This is usually how managers become 'experienced'. They learn from their errors. Since it does not always follow that 'success' is directly associated with the diagnosis and the remedy prescribed, much could be learned by investigating the reasons for 'success'. Due to pressure of circumstances this is rarely done, and hardly ever in a systematic way. Because of that some opportunities to 'learn by experience' are lost.

What we have been describing is a process of reasoning by a responsible person from the experience of 'pain' to a point where action is taken to relieve it. The action almost always involves other people who may or may not have been involved in the reasoning process and the process of reaching a decision to act involves the manager in a set of relationships with others including typically those who report the difficulty, those upon whose evidence the definition of the problem so crucially depends, and those who take action to resolve it. The manager might also feel that there could be advantages in sharing his thoughts with those closest to him and in seeking opinions from experienced people outside that group. Or he may look outside his organisation for experts who may know whether ready-made tested solutions are available which would save him the time and trouble of learning by his own experience, although the dangers in this have already been mentioned. Some other difficulties of problem-definition and diagnosis are described in the text, and in the cases we have included to exemplify our method.

The second process has to do with the way people of different ranks and responsibilities, with different special competences and experience of the organisation, with perhaps different degrees of commitment, and faced perhaps with different difficulties and ways of perceiving problems, relate to each other during the sequences in which problems are diagnosed, planned and implemented. It also has to do with the way these relationships are ordered and managed and by whom, and for what ends and for whose benefit. These are matters that raise much theoretical and practical controversy. It would be difficult to deny, however, the existence of a connection between the way relationships are ordered and success or failure in effecting changes that are designed to improve matters.

Lupton–Tanner method

Our approach to the management of change rests entirely on a particular view of *the second process*. The decision to adopt it requires at least a suspension of scepticism; at most whole-hearted commitment. It is necessary, therefore, at this stage briefly to state our view, compare it with other views and show how the rational process and our version of what may be called the 'social process' may fruitfully be combined. We can then go on to outline our method and our treatment of it in this book, before getting down to detail.

Rationale for involvement The idea of involving a wider constituency in the process of managing change should not, in our view, be adopted as a concession to pressure from below, or as an expression of the personal beliefs of powerful people about organisational democracy. We believe that to involve as many people as possible as deeply as possible is the only sensible way to proceed. We say 'as deeply as possible' advisedly. Time and effort devoted to wide and deep involvement attract economic costs which must be balanced against possible economic benefits. In our society managers are expected to initiate change, to take responsibility for what happens and also to decide on the extent and level of involvement of others. Our advice to them is to err on the side of too much rather than too little, too deep rather than too superficial, involvement. If a manager judges that there are serious obstacles to wide and deep involvement the onus should be on him to explain to others who may wish to be involved the grounds on which his judgement rests.

We shall describe what we mean by 'deep involvement'. We certainly do not mean 'tell and sell', where a small group of senior managers assisted by specialists follows a mainly rational process of relating means to ends (often foreshortened with the help of intuitive leaps) and arrives at a decision about what has to be done if the things that they as managers are interested in are to be improved. Aware that other organisation members might have other interests and might not regard what is being suggested as improvement, they now see the need to tell these others and in the process persuade them at best to fall enthusiastically into line, at worst to accept inducements not to obstruct. To the extent that in the rational process the interests and objectives of others have been carefully investigated and incorporated, that the proposals are carefully explained, and that the explainers are trusted, then the proposals may be 'bought'. There is no guarantee, however, that what is 'bought' is 'owned' in the sense that the 'buyer' is enthusiastically committed to the 'product'. There could well be difficulties when, during implementation, the implications of just what has been 'bought' begin to be fully appreciated. As we argue later (pp. 88–89) this is nonetheless a frequently attempted short cut in the process which we are advocating.

We do not enthuse much either over what we call 'propose and bargain'. In this case managers may work out in some detail a number of possible ways of reaching objectives which they know or suspect will not be palatable to other groups. They will then either choose one of the alternatives or disclose them all and ask other groups to choose the ground for negotiation. In neither case is the development of joint commitment to an agreed objective possible. The best that can be hoped for is that the pursuit of the manager's objectives will not be obstructed, and that the costs of removing some of the obstructions will be known to him in advance of implementation. Some elements of 'tell and sell' may be found in situations of 'propose and bargain'. In so far as the proposals have been carefully prepared in detail, and in the bargaining process the difficulties are explored frankly and in detail, and each party trusts the other to keep its word, then the bargaining process may produce a degree of common purpose and commitment. However, it is in the nature of bargaining to take up opposing stances and to use information as a counter, disclosing it only as tactics require. Even 'win–win' bargaining to joint decision does not make joint commitment to action certain.

We may distinguish a third way in which managers might approach the management of change and call it 'winning consent by consultation'. This involves managers 'roughing out' a programme for change and then asking others to comment in detail and make suggestions for improvement in the programme. In this way fresh information and ideas may be incorporated and the programme adapted. The revised version may now be put to the same audience for further comment until the manager feels that he can confidently proceed in the knowledge that the objectives have been consented to and much new knowledge and long experience have gone into the planning process. The weakness in this method lies in the assumptions it makes about the willingness of people to contribute their experience and knowledge. The extent of their willingness may relate to their confidence that their helpfulness will not be exploited to their disadvantage.

None of these three approaches, and the combinations of them that are frequently met with, do much to spread more widely responsibility for the outcomes of planned change. But that is not such a serious criticism of them as that the way they structure the social process inhibits the free input of information and ideas. The rational process needs free input to produce efficient solutions, so we need a social

process that will ensure free input but which does not at
the same time confuse or obstruct the rational process. That
is what our method does.

Lupton–Tanner method in outline   The alternative we have
evolved takes the form of a step-by-step process for generating
agreement about the improvements to be aimed at, about
how the improvements are to be achieved and why, about
who will make them and how those involved may jointly
learn from the experience of having been involved.
   The main steps are as follows.

1   *To pool the knowledge and experience of the members
    of an organisational unit, and to arrive through discussion
    at an agreed and well defined aim.* We define members
    not only as those whose formal roles require them to
    initiate, plan and be responsible for the implementation
    of change, but also those whose work is likely to be
    affected (directly and/or indirectly) by changes in the
    setting in which that work is done, and the way it is
    required to be done.

2   *To list those items which, in the opinion of those whose
    experience and knowledge is being tapped, have potential
    influence upon the agreed aim if it is to be achieved
    within a given time.* It is essential during this step to
    resist the temptation to omit items in the interests of
    simplicity; it is a variety-generating exercise. The search
    for simplicity comes later. At this stage everyone in
    the organisational unit is an 'organisation member',
    although not all will, or indeed can possibly be, directly
    and continuously involved.

3   *To follow, still in a group setting, a series of diagnostic
    procedures the result of which is a shortlist of items to
    be changed if the aim is to be achieved, a commitment
    by everyone to that list, and a plan which states who
    will see that the changes are made, and how the plan
    and its outcomes will be monitored.*

4   *To check whether the actual outcomes deviated from the*

planned outcomes and to learn by doing so to improve the processes of aiming, planning and changing.

Plan of the book

Chapters 1, 2 and 3, which describe the procedures, each have three parts. The first sets out in detail, and with illustrative material, one or more steps of the method. This is followed by a brief theoretical justification. The third part describes some of the difficulties that may be encountered in using the method and suggests how they can be overcome.

Those whose immediate interest is in the mastery of the method itself may, on first reading, choose to skip the theory parts and return to them later. However, it would be unwise to ignore them altogether. To question Why? as well as to know How? is to be equipped the better to learn from experience.

Special attention should be given to the last part of each chapter. This is where we report the results of our experience of using the method as a means of planning and making improvements, and of organisational learning.

In Chapter 4 the contribution of our method to continuous organisational learning is examined and in Chapter 5 we discuss some approaches to the choice of objectives.

1 Making a start

All objectives need a plan for their realisation and all plans posit change. Planning involves people and people are affected when changes are made. This chapter describes the first systematic steps in planning for change, including

- the logical and social processes involved in deriving items to be changed if a quantified objective is to be realised in a given time, and

- the transformation of the items into dimensioned variables in preparation for the next stages of mapping directions for change.

Setting the objective

In a later chapter we suggest some procedures for choosing an objective. For the present we will assume that an objective has been agreed, insisting only that whatever it is it must be expressed as a quantity with a given time period for its achievement. Unless and until this is done it is difficult to start plan-making using the Lupton–Tanner method. Three examples from our experience illustrate what is meant by 'quantity' and 'time-period'.

1   The top management of a large commercial business after lengthy consideration of their past history and

some future scenarios prepared by their corporate planning department decided that they should aim to double their return on assets in seven years.

2   An education authority group aimed to increase the number of children remaining at school after age 15 in a particular part of the region, from 35% to 80% in five years. This was a little more ambitious than the politicians at the Town Hall were demanding.

3   When the personnel managers of the British divisions and plants of a multi-national company assembled to prepare a plan to increase the visibility and credibility of the personnel function amongst line managers they experienced some difficulty in translating the regard of other people into a quantity. However, it was better to attempt that than abandon it. What about a graduated scale with 'nil credibility' at one end and 'complete credibility' at the other? and another scale with 'nil visibility' and 'complete visibility' at the extremities? A point could be marked on each representing their view of the present condition and another which showed where they thought they could reasonably be in x years time. To find some kind of quantity to go with the full scale provides the reference points which as we shall see are essential to the plan-making process and to the implementation and monitoring of plans.

In this chapter we begin the search for a plan to achieve the objective.

We recommend or rather, insist, that the fullest use possible be made of the relevant knowledge of people who experience uniquely and in detail the functioning of the organisational unit to be changed. Their experience may be limited, but matters of great significance may be missed if it goes unrecorded. If successful management is, among other things, 'scrupulous attention to detail' then the management of change especially must rigorously adhere to that principle. In planning changes the collection of detailed information must be done with great thoroughness. The detail must be assembled systematically and participatively so that whatever programme of change is decided upon, it will not only be based on all the evidence and experience available, but will also command general support and commitment. In this chapter we show how to assemble an agreed list of items to be changed, and how to transform them into variables which can be expressed as one or more dimensions.

Generating variety

In these early stages of our procedure we are deliberately generating as much variety as we can, so that every item and every connection between items that may be of possible relevance to planning and implementing a programme to achieve the objective is included. Later we shall reduce the variety in a systematic way to arrive at a simple step-by-step programme of change. Our 'philosophy' then demands pain-staking and systematic exploration of the knowledge and experience of organisation members by organisation members themselves, *via* representative groups. External 'experts' may be useful to help things along especially in the early stages, as adjuncts to the do-it-yourself process.

We know what the objective is. Each member should now go away from the group, reflect on his own experience and knowledge, and that of colleagues, and write a comprehensive list of those elements of the system under consideration as he sees it which have to be attended to if the objective is to be reached in the stated time. When looking at a system we are concerned with the interconnectedness of all elements. The difficulty is where to draw the boundary. In a practical sense the system is defined as including those elements which lie within the control or influence of the decision-makers or those they advise that are relevant to the objective. Any one of these should be capable of change. No judgements should be made at this stage about priorities.

Items for change

Let us for the moment step into the role of a personnel

manager, who may be a member of a group similar to the one described above, with the task of drawing up the agenda for change. Let us also suppose that the agreed objective is to reduce unit cost by 5% in one year. The personnel and industrial relations manager's experience might lead him to draw up a list of items such as:

1   Labour turnover among skilled maintenance fitters.

2   Rate of absenteeism among semi-skilled operators.

3   Procedures for selection and skill training of operators.

4   Trade union demarcation lines.

5   Supervisory style.

6   Procedures for processing worker grievances.

7   Shiftwork system.

8   Overtime working.

9   Administration of wage payment system.

10   Design of wage system.

11   Wage and salary structures.

12   Restrictive work practices.

13   Management structure.

14   Management style.

15   Worker motivation.

There are, so far, fifteen items. In our experience personnel specialists asked to name all the possible items of behaviour that might be associated with the unit cost of a product or service will think of many more, including possibly the behaviour of shop stewards, and the way transfers and promotions are handled. Not to mention those from other specialist areas: material costs, energy costs, material utilisation, etc.

As an exercise in drawing up lists of items of this kind the reader should imagine some improvement he would like to see in his own organisation, express it quantitatively, and jot down as many items as he can think of.

Private and public agenda for change

It is, we emphasise, not advisable at this stage to arrange the items in order of priority, although there is a natural desire to do so. It is evident if one observes the behaviour and listens to the talk of people who work in organisations, that everyone has his/her own general priorities for change. They usually are single items, at most a few, expressed in phrases like 'If I were the general manager the first thing I would do would be to make some radical changes in the salary structure' or 'If I had a spare man with the right experience the first thing I would do would be to tackle the problem of the brain drain from the company'. Sometimes priorities are revealed by activity rather than words as when workers who experience the administration of the wage system as unfair manipulate the booking of their work. Their priority is to establish equity (as they define it) in the effort-reward relationship, and they act accordingly.

General priorities of this kind are related to general values like efficiency or fairness. Their emergence and existence may plausibly be explained as the end result of a largely intuitive process, strongly influenced by the need to find simple ways to interpret, explain and cope with complexity. In the course of time long lists of possible priorities are reduced to shorter lists or single items dear to the heart of the intuitor. The process by which the lists 'in the head' came to be there, the extent to which they represent a comprehensive description of the realities of individual experience, and the logics used to evaluate and select are not usually open to external scrutiny. Indeed the individual may not know how to make them explicit. Our method encourages and makes possible the public exposure of these intuitive processes. However, we recommend that the search for agreement on priorities should be left until everyone's long lists are 'on the table'. Our method is designed expressly to facilitate the listing of priorities for action linked to a single quantified improvement objective. Our aim is to avoid the revelation of individual

priorities relating to disparate general values and aims,
whether they be personal or departmental, for example,
'controlling costs' or 'caring for people'.

Back to the group

Each individual member now brings his list to the group
meeting. Each reads out the items and explains why he has
included them, that is, how they relate to the objective. Others
will be expected to ask questions. It is crucial that the questions are framed as enquiries to increase the enlightenment
of everyone. The aim is not to use the opportunity to persuade
others to cross things off their list, *nor* to parade specialised
knowledge, *nor* to advocate change programmes prematurely,
nor to use formal authority to silence others, *nor* to conceal
facts or ideas as a way of gaining political advantage or
psychological protection. Our procedure does not at any stage
encourage blocking gambits like 'everybody knows that the
organisation of our Tool Room is rubbish, I've been saying
it for years'. Rather it stresses agreement to a specific objective
and then seeks to find out what has to be changed and in
what sequence to reach it. Maybe the reorganisation of the
Tool Room will emerge high on the list of priorities *after*
the procedure is complete, maybe not. When all have had
their say and have responded to questions, everyone will have
a much more comprehensive view of the nature of the system
they are planning to change. At the end of this stage there
will be a long list of possible items for change. There will
also have been some preliminary discussion of possible priorities but it is advisable to limit such discussion at this stage
for reasons that will soon become apparent.

Dimensions

The next task for the group is to transform the items on
the long list into an even longer list of variables expressed
as dimensions, the current state of which can be placed on
a scale on which changes or projected changes may be plotted.
In everyday discussion people are accustomed to talk rather

loosely of, for example 'the way we do our planning' or 'the wage payment system'. These ways of referring to things act as labels for a potentially large number of detailed aspects of the item. What we must do, if our technique is to have its full value, is to 'unpack' these items and make very clear the particular dimensions of each that are to be considered in the planning process. The reasons for this essential but difficult and time-consuming process will reveal themselves once it has been started. Our experience is that the reasons are readily accepted. The difficulty arises because people find the very idea of dimensions difficult to accept for so-called 'subjective' items. However, some form of measurement is necessary so that the group can express with some precision their view about the present state of the system that is to be changed and to plot the magnitude of the changes that have to be made to achieve the objective.

To exemplify: the group might start with some items relating to employee turnover, where records already exist and where variations are already plotted. The dimensions in this case could be represented as scales measuring turnover rates for various categories of employees. Our personnel specialist thought that turnover of skilled maintenance fitters was related to the objective of reduced unit cost. A scale for that variable could show zero at one end and 100% at the other as annual turnover rates. A cross could be placed on the scale showing the current position as derived from personnel records, as in Figure 1.1.

0%   100

Figure 1.1   Dimension 1: Turnover of maintenance fitters

Another dimension related to decisions to stay with the organisation or leave it is *labour stability*. It is possible for the rate of turnover to be high as measured on Dimension 1, while stability is high also. That is: turnover might take place because a lot of short-term stayers come and go throughout the year while the bulk of the employees decide to stay. Stability could be measured on a scale expressing what percentage of the labour force at the start of a year have remained to the end, as shown in Figure 1.2.

Figure 1.2   Dimension 2: Stability of maintenance fitter labour force

In the examples just discussed measurement is relatively easy and there will be records available to allow the X's on the dimensions to be placed without much conflict of opinion. Other items may be, and often are, less straight-forward. How, for example, can the way that worker grievances are processed be measured? Some aspects of this are easy. For each category of grievance and each category of employee we could measure annual incidence, such as how many grievances there are each year about pay. Among invoice clerks, for example, or among supervisors, as in Figure 1.3. The number on the right of the scales is unimportant, as long as it allows the placing of a cross. The placing of the cross is again made possible by reference to personnel records.

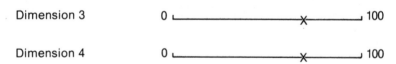

Figure 1.3   Pay grievances – annual incidence. Dimension 3: Invoice clerks; Dimension 4: Supervisors

The efficiency of the grievance procedures is probably as relevant to the objective as is their incidence. The group may decide that efficiency can be represented by three scales, one representing the time taken to deal with the grievance, the second expressing the satisfaction of the aggrieved party with the outcome, the third the satisfaction of the party at the receiving end of the complaint. These can be clearly seen in Figures 1.4–1.6.

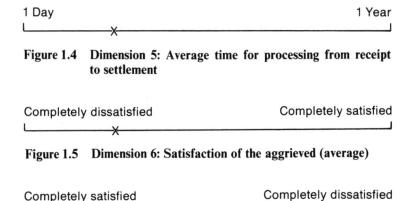

Figure 1.4   **Dimension 5: Average time for processing from receipt to settlement**

Figure 1.5   **Dimension 6: Satisfaction of the aggrieved (average)**

Figure 1.6   **Dimension 7: Satisfaction of recipients**

The reader will probably have noticed that the variables and scales are, in the case of 'subjective' items, derived from those characteristics of the item which are ordinarily the stuff of everyday discussion about it. When people in companies are talking about grievances and how they are, or ought to be, dealt with they usually refer to How many? How long? How satisfied? They may also refer to the degree of formality, and might want a scale to represent such a dimension, on which to record judgements about how formal the procedures for processing grievances currently are, and which direction of change is consistent with the objective.

Scales and judgements

In our work with groups in organisations of various kinds we have found that to derive dimensions from the items is the part of the procedure that they find most difficult. So much so as in some cases to want to abandon it and work only with the items. We have already hinted at a method to overcome the difficulties. Dimensions may be derived from an item by first listing the characteristics of the item usually referred to when it is being described or judged. Then a scale can be devised to represent the characteristic. By way of illustration take another item in our personnel specialist's list – 'the way our pay system is designed'. Instead of asking what the particular features of that existing scheme are we ask instead 'what do people say about pay systems in general, which they then use to judge a particular system?'. We will then find that people tend to talk about complexity, equity (as perceived), formality (by reference to paper work, committees, etc), and already we have three possible variables and scales to represent dimensions. We refer now to Figures 1.7–1.9, and to Case study 1 which follows.

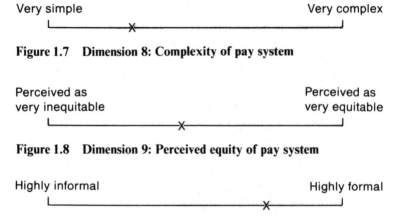

Figure 1.7   Dimension 8: Complexity of pay system

Figure 1.8   Dimension 9: Perceived equity of pay system

Figure 1.9   Dimension 10: Formality of pay system

Case study 1   Dimensioning

An example of the generation of variables and their dimensioning is provided by a group of senior managers from a foodstuffs manufacturing company. Their objective was to consider how they could achieve a 25% increase in profits during the following year. The discussions quickly produced a list of items which they felt to be relevant to the objective.

Objective: 25% increase in profits in 1 year.

- Increase domestic sales.
- Increase exports.
- Increase labour productivity.
- More effective use of material resources.
- Eliminate waste.
- Reduction in general expenses.
- Minimise product cost.
- Change pricing policy.
- Better prices for raw materials.
- Reconsider advertising policy.
- Reconsider distribution channels.
- Change motivation rewards system.
-- Reconsider sources of financing.
- Reorganisation and change in structure.
- New products: reconsider product line.

It was clear that this list needed quite a lot of consideration in order to generate a set of dimensions which would be precise and clear enough to facilitate the later stages of the Lupton–Tanner process. In this respect it was quite typical of the sort of list which is produced at this stage. The group therefore set about the task of seeking out the dimensions associated with each of the items in the list. This can be illustrated by reference to some of the results.

Under the heading 'Distribution channels' the group included the dimensions shown in Figure 1.10.

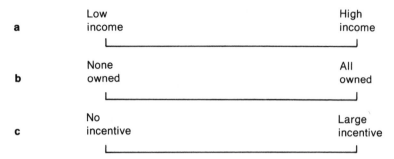

Figure 1.10 (a) Potential customers. (b) Ownership of means of distribution. (c) Distributor incentives

In the ensuing discussion it was agreed that the scales for (a) and (c) needed to be revised to make them more readily measured and to remove the subjectivity implicit in the judgement of high/low scales. The dimensions shown in Figure 1.11 were those finally accepted.

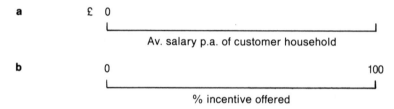

Figure 1.11   (a) Potential customers. (b) Distributor incentives

Similar attention was paid to all of the items in the list. Some of the resulting dimensions and their initial scales are listed in Figure 1.12.

These are just some examples from the expanded list which the group generated in the process of dimensioning the items which they had first suggested to be of relevance to the objective. In most of these cases it was a relatively straightforward matter to amend the first scaling suggestions in such a way that the meaning became quite clear to all. The last of those listed above, the dimension concerned with organisation structure, was less easily dealt with. The scale as offered was not suitable because it begged the question as to what was meant by 'well organised'. This might have as many interpretations as there were members

1 Utilisation of material resources

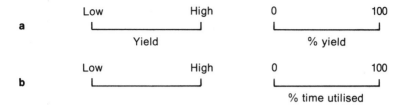

2 Advertising

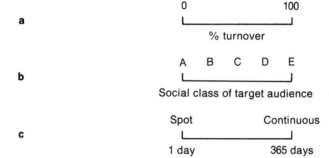

3 Organisation

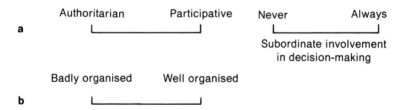

Figure 1.12 Resulting dimensions for Case study 1. 1. Utilisation of material resources: (a) utilisation of raw materials, (b) utilisation of machinery. 2. Advertising: (a) cost, (b) quality, (c) frequency. 3. Organisation: (a) decision-making process, (b) organisation structure

of the group. In any case it does not have the characteristics of objectivity and openness to measurement which we seek in the dimensioning process. After a long discussion during which many of the aspects of organisation were identified, a set of dimensions was added to the final list which collectively addressed this problem of appropriate organisation.

After having placed a cross on each dimension in the manner previously described the group must also make a judgement about the direction of movement along each dimension which would aid progress towards the objective. This may be indicated by an arrow along the dimension. This assignment of an arrow to determine the desired direction to move a particular variable can give rise to difficulties. Members of the group may find it impossible to decide which direction of movement is consistent with the adopted objective. Occasionally people will feel that they do not want to move along the dimension at all or that movement in either direction seems consistent with improvement.

A graphical analysis of this stage of the process will help us to see why this can be the case. Our process assumes that for all of the variables over the range of interest to us there is a linear relationship between the objective and the variable. If we plot this as a graph in which the vertical axis represents increasing degrees of achievement of the objective (for example, profit) and the horizontal axis represents the dimension of the variables, we have, for example, the analysis shown in Figure 1.13.

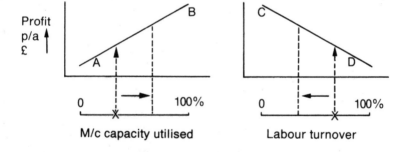

Figure 1.13   Analysis of variable/objective relationship
Note: the lines AB and CD represent the relationships between the variables and the objectives. Their slope represents the 'potency' of the variables as discussed in Chapter 2

This linearity is an assumption which serves well enough in most cases. However, if we do have information which suggests some other form of relationship, that should be used in preference. This most frequently comes to light when someone says, 'I do not see any point in moving this variable – it is just as we want it'. Graphically this implies a curve of the form (a) and (b) illustrated in Figure 1.14. In (a) a move in either direction leads to a reduction in the objective and is therefore unwanted. In (b) movement of any magnitude in either direction yields no advantage and again there would be no point in attempting to change it. By contrast (c) offers equal advantage to movement in either direction. The choice here may be determined by the relative ease with which change may be affected in each of the directions.

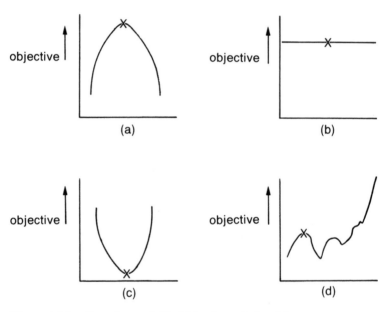

Figure 1.14   Complex variable/objective relationships

More complex curvilinear relationships between dimensions and the objective are obviously possible and, if known, can be considered in the same way. In the example of (d) we would require a large movement along the dimension from the point marked because the initial outcome of a small change is to reduce the level of the objective. The expectation of the eventual rewards to this change would outweigh the immediate negative effects. The arrow should indicate a move from left to right.

There is another trap for the unwary in drawing arrows which may be exemplified by reference to the dimensions for 'pay system' (see p. 18). Some people have a general preference for the simplicity, equity, and informality they represent. We number ourselves among them. But (and here is the trap) it does not necessarily follow that if we rearrange our pay system design to bring it in line with our personal preferences we will contribute to the objective of reduced unit cost. It could just be that a scheme of greater complexity, more formally administered, and perceived as more inequitable might be more appropriate. The discipline of testing one's preferences by reference to logic and the evidence is not, as we have discovered in our work, highly developed among managers, supervisors, and union members and officials in general. It is essential that it be learned by members of the group as they go through the labour of transforming items to dimensions. If the group allows the personal preferences of specialists, or of those with formal power to overrule logic and the facts, then much of the point of our method is lost. That is why there must develop in the group an openness to logic and evidence and a willingness and capacity to be moved by them.

At the end of this stage the group will have produced a list of dimensions. For some of them it will have been fairly straightforward to assign a cross showing the current position, the labour turnover variables being a good example. In that case the group may have quickly reached agreement about the position of the arrow head. With other dimensions the positioning of crosses and arrows will be a source of disagreement among members of the group. Some ideas and processes for resolving such disagreements will be described in Chapter 2.

The output from the work of individuals and the group as described in this chapter should be a numbered list of dimensions on all of which there are crosses and arrows. In our experience the list for an objective such as reduction of unit cost might number over one hundred. In our personnel example earlier in this chapter we derived at least 10 variables from 3 items. Our list of 10 could be represented in the manner shown in Figure 1.15. We have called these 'dimensioned variables' for obvious reasons. (In what follows we will mainly use the term 'variable' as a shorthand.)

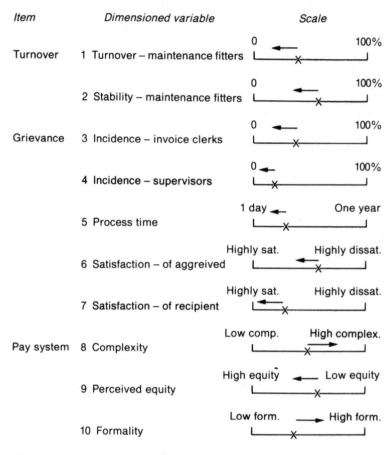

Figure 1.15   Example of dimensioned variables

We have just finished describing a lengthy, time-consuming, fairly difficult, and certainly unfamiliar process. From our original list of *items*, (as painstakingly compiled) we have added further variety in the form of an even longer numbered list of *dimensioned variables*. As if that were not enough we started the process of placing crosses and arrows on the scales. If we asked a single individual to do the whole job, it would consume a great deal of that person's time and energy. For reasons already rehearsed we insist that the job be done by a group, and a group so composed as to emphasise differences in personal experience and occupational perspective. Such a mixture is certain to give rise to sometimes uncomfortable conflicts of viewpoint and interpretation of the facts, adding to the time and energy consumed. It is necessary, therefore, to justify taking up so much of the time of people who could have been doing more familiar, less uncomfortable tasks and would probably have preferred that. The question is: are the results going to be worth the time taken and the effort expended?

Is the effort worthwhile?

We offer two answers. The *first* is based on our observations on the way organisations and those who work in them usually handle the technical, economic, social and psychological variety they generate in the process of responding to changing circumstances in the market place and in the context of broader currents of law and opinion. We observe top managers attempting to reduce variety by dividing it up and allocating the parts to specialised divisions, functional departments, and hierarchical layers. The effect of this is that the top managers are not exposed to variety but to simpler versions of reality, largely the result of detail having been filtered through the layers and *via* the coded communications of the specialised management professions. The top manager from his 'helicopter' sees a simpler pattern, and works with a 'model' based on it to inform his judgement and decisions. The various layers have each their own simplified and different 'model' – middle management, supervision, shop floor, office floor; and so have the specialists – manufacturing, finance and accounting, personnel, marketing and sales, research and development. Of course there are some shared 'models' and viewpoints, otherwise the co-ordination of the specialised departments, divisions and layers would be extremely difficult. *Our procedure may be regarded as part of that process of co-ordination*, but differing in purpose and *modus operandi* from the devices more commonly used, such as committees, liaison persons and departments, project groups and, significantly, formal authority and formal control systems. These are set up to deal with structural fragmentation by structural overlays and authority-reinforcing devices. If they encourage the pooling of knowledge and information the motive will probably be to increase the power of particular groups to influence events in their favour. Our procedure has a different motive. It is designed for the unfamiliar task of making knowledge and experience more generally and openly available, and to direct it towards agreed objectives for organisational improvement. Innovations of this kind always encounter inertia, hence the need to take time, and to take pains, to generate a *common* body of knowledge and a *common model*; not merely as a theoretical exercise, but as a means to particular organisational ends. This particular innovation may be regarded as a permanent addition to the organisation 'culture', a counter to the processes of structural fragmentation that accompany growing size and complexity. A few days spent mapping the variety seems a small price to pay for a gain of that kind.

The *second*, and related, reason for generating variety is more technical. It is designed to lay the essential foundation for subsequent steps in the procedure which are designed to *reduce* variety. As we evolve our plan for change it will become apparent that the dimensioned variables will help us to ask questions about how *potent* each variable is in relation to the objective, such as 'what would happen to the objective if the variable were moved in the direction of the arrow?', and, just as necessary for our purposes, to reach a view about what *blockages* might confront us if we were to attempt to alter the variable. Without the scales it would be difficult to focus the attention of everyone on the possible consequences for the objective of changing the variables. To the extent that we fail in that, so will our chances of producing simple, effective and agreed programmes for change recede.

Why mixed-discipline teams?

We have found it difficult to convince some senior managers of the value of a mixed-level-mixed-discipline team, seconded from their usual work for long periods, whose purpose is to work carefully through the procedures we have developed for planning change. They are attracted sometimes by the idea of working in systematic ways towards solutions to problems, but prefer to have the work done for them by a single person, or a specialised department. Usually the senior manager after discussions with his colleagues will set the objectives. The task of developing a plan, or alternative plans, is then assigned. At that point we have found interest among senior managers in the technical aspects of our procedure which might be seen as more logical, factually more wide ranging and procedurally more thorough than others, and in this mode posing no threat to established ways. The senior manager is still in personal control of the process of objective-setting and plan-making, and free to accept, reject or modify the suggestions of subordinates, finding justification in the doctrine of 'the buck stops here'.

Others have been attracted by the team-building potential of our procedure, and see the technical procedures as a means to that end. Typically, they prefer mixed-discipline to mixed-level groups, and more often than not, want to bring peace and a sense of common purpose to unruly factions at the level below them. Those who take this view never wish to be closely involved with the group, so that they too remain free to veto or modify. We refer now to Case study 2.

Case study 2   Team building; the importance of the setting

The manager of a mass production plant was experiencing problems in the assembly of a particular product. This product was
produced in sufficient volume to have its own assembly line which
was sited in a separate bay of a large assembly factory. The
problems were reducing the productivity of this assembly line
to such a degree that the plant manager was determined to take
whatever steps were necessary to put things right. In discussions
with him it soon became apparent that there were many competing
explanations for this lack of productivity: each of his subordinates
preferring a version which laid the greater part of the responsibility
for the shortcomings with others in the management team.

It was agreed that the consultants should work with the plant
manager and all of his immediate subordinates and their assistants
using the Lupton–Tanner technique in an attempt to isolate the
primary factors in the productivity problem. In this way it was
hoped not only to identify and act upon the important variables
in the productivity problem but also to begin the process of building
a consensual view of the task which would encourage the management team to work with rather than against each other.

The managers were brought together for a two-day seminar
workshop. After a brief introduction to the technique, they
embarked on the processes of variable generation and cross-
impact assessment.* The group included the deputy plant
manager, the maintenance engineer, the quality controller, the
personnel and industrial relations manager, the procurement
manager and the financial controller.

The broad objective of the exercise was known to everyone,
that is, to find ways of working together to improve productivity,
and the group had few problems in deciding to aim for a 5%
increase in output per man hour in each of the next two years.
The meetings of the group took place in the plant. Those present
knew what the general idea was, but knew little about what to
expect in detail. Their previous experience of consultants was
that the managers provided the information, the consultants did
the work of diagnosis and provided solutions. Now the managers
not only provided the information, they also did the work of
diagnosis and providing solutions, the role of the consultants being
to provide the method and help the process along.

The process itself was hampered by the fact that, contrary to

---

*Cross-impact assessment is the final step in the Lupton–Tanner
procedure. It is described in detail in Chapter 3.

the consultants' advice, the two-day meeting was held in working hours and adjacent to the plant. As a result there were far too many interruptions as now this and now that manager was called away to resolve some short-term crisis in the plant. This did not, we think, affect the nature of the solution reached – people had ample opportunity to ensure that their brief absences did not result in our overlooking some item of importance – but it did weaken the process of team building and the strength of the consensus reached.

Quite apart from these disruptions other more central difficulties had to be overcome. The meeting was initially stormy and argumentative as each of the participants in turn sought to establish his view of the situation and deny others. The consultants' role in this early stage was that of referee. It was important that these differing points of view were brought out but it was equally important that their evaluation should be removed from the level of petty political points-scoring to a reasoned collective judgement of the facts which were available.

Given a firmness in chairing these early stages and an even handed treatment of all participants, it was possible to move to a more impersonal, analytical search for the factors which impinged on the problem.

The final list of factors numbered fifty items. The selection of these items reproduced in the following list serves to indicate the level of detail which this study involved. The precision with which dimensions could be specified for this problem was of great value in the analysis of the problem.

List of variables and their dimensions

1	Component matching	unmatched components as % of supply.
2	Stock; components	number available.
3	Faulty components	% of total supply.
4	Component delivery	% builds lost for supply failure.
5	Electrical breakdown	% machine time running.
6	Organisation of Mtce	extent of centralisation.
7	Supply of electronic experts	number of men available.
8	Batch size	number of products per shift.
9	Variation in component specification	% components non-standard.
10	Labour stability	level on Bowey index.

11	Wasted time	% available time.
12	Operator training; induction	hours/man.
13	Working conditions; noise	decibels.
14	Sabotage	% assemblies lost.
15	Space	sq. metres.

This was possible because of the intimate knowledge of the system under study possessed collectively by those who were taking part. The complete list represented the combined view of all the specialists involved as to the variables which could affect the productivity of the assembly line.

Within the two days set aside for this exercise it was possible, in spite of the interruptions, to determine the list of variables, assess their potency, identify possible blockages to change and make considerable progress in the completion of the cross-impact matrix. Everyone learned that for such a complex operation two interrupted days are not nearly enough for serious team building and organisational integration or for making plans to achieve objectives and generating enthusiasm for them. Remarkably though, enough was done to show the potential of the method despite the unpropitious circumstances.

We cannot insist that the way described in Case study 2 of using the procedures we have devised are unacceptable. We have willingly and knowingly collaborated with senior managers who were less interested in specific programmes for change, than in the building of a more cohesive management team which would use the same information base. We have also helped to train a group of young specialists from a management services department to follow the technical steps of the procedure. In this case the interest in team building was subordinate to the acquisition of a new mode of organisational diagnosis to add to the tool kit of a management services group. However, we can and do insist that the full advantages of what we are proposing are best gained when the technique and the team building are integrated. Otherwise, the strength of commitment to agreed programmes may be sapped.

The difficulties

By now some of the difficulties will have become apparent. Most of them, we find, stem from uncertainties about how to deal with the unfamiliar. We can mention and exemplify some of those that especially attend that stage of our procedure which deals with the translation of items into dimensioned variables.

Each member of a typical mixed-discipline management group will feel secure within the confines of his specialism and his job description. The first stages of the procedure, that is, listing and comparing items for change, do not trespass on his territory. Indeed, the specialist may welcome the opportunity to explain to others why the items within his sphere of formal responsibility are significant for the achievement of the objective. When it comes to finding dimensioned variables, however, details have to be considered that lie outside the specialist's occupational field of vision or his formal span of authority and responsibility. What is seen by the designers and initiators of the exercise as an opportunity for everyone to learn from everyone else could well be (and has been observed to be) seen by some participants as an invitation to others both to poach on their job territory and to ask awkward laymen's questions about covert professional mysteries. This is one explanation for the politely defensive behaviour that is often displayed at this stage. If there are trade union officers involved, they and the managers might see the discussion about variables and dimensions as a vehicle for gathering information that might later be used to beat the 'opposition' in bargaining sessions, and this will affect the openness with which information is exchanged and issues discussed. In short, it is inevitable that traditional modes of working and relating will be carried into the group. To the extent that these are 'political', competitive (for the boss's favours, for career progression and so on), and authoritarian, and not helpful, caring, co-operative and open, so will these kinds of difficulties arise.

This is why whoever is the senior manager who starts the process off must see it *not* as an experiment to be shut down if it is not, by his criteria, succeeding. If the news gets around that this is how it is regarded then the participants will play around with the new 'fashion' so as to speed its demise. Rather, those involved must be encouraged to regard it as the first move in a permanent shift in management style and organisation culture. The senior manager must himself demonstrate his commitment to such a shift, explain his reasons for encouraging and lead by the example of being himself as open, caring, co-operative and supportive as he can possibly be. He must also see that the group includes someone who can facilitate the transition through unmapped territory to a different culture, but not abdicate to the facilitator his own responsibilities. To emphasise now the importance of team building we refer to the following Case study.

Case study 3 Formulating strategy and team-building

Newly promoted from being a Divisional Head, the Chief Executive of a large European Bank planned a three-day 'retreat' at which together with his senior colleagues he could chart future directions for the Bank, lay plans and gain commitment.

At the suggestion of the Personnel Director one of the authors was invited to help as a facilitator. The group of senior colleagues who gathered at a country hotel included the Chief Executive, the Heads of the major Divisions of the Bank and the Finance Director and Personnel Director.

The remit of the facilitator as agreed at a prior meeting with the Chief Executive and the Personnel Director was to live and work with the group over the whole three days and to try to ensure that as far as possible:

1   the discussions were open and frank,

2   personal incompatabilities and divisional vested interests did not become obstacles to co-operation, and

3   the group would be moulded into a powerful and purposeful team of strategic collaborators, prepared to influence their subordinates to participate in and implement sub-plans within the agreed plan; or at least to start that process.

There was to be no formal agenda, nor premeditated structure for the proceedings, but it must have been clear to everyone concerned that from their previous knowledge the new chief's style would be very different from that of his predecessor. At least a good deal less authoritarian and unpredictable.

There was some pleasant skirmishing after the group assembled reflecting a long-established pattern of relationships but affected by the fact that a peer was now the boss. It was suggested that the procedure developed by Lupton and Tanner be used, at least at the start, to aid the process. This was readily accepted, perhaps to allay the uneasiness at the lack of structure, and after a short explanation of the procedure, the group started the search for a single objective for the Bank that could be quantified and to which they could all subscribe.

Most of the first day was spent on this task, during which there were wide ranging discussions, for example about the competitive situation of the Bank past, present, and future, in its parts and as a whole, as well as its past and potential performance. There

were many telephone calls to Head Office for statistical information. It was decided that Return on Investment was the best overall
measure of the Bank's performance and the objective agreed was
'to improve ROI by x% in y years'. The detailed arguments around
the x and y quantities gave each member of the group a closer
insight into the problems of functions and divisions other than
their own and helped cement relationships. Previously unrecog-
nised sources of conflict and sub-optimisation came to the surface
and were dealt with in a process in which the facilitator had a
significant part.

The following day each member prepared his own list of items
for change and these were exhaustively discussed. It became
apparent that there would be no time to complete the dimensioning
process, so it was decided to use the items themselves as the
basis for scoring on potency for the identification of blockages,
and for cross-impact analysis. The members of the group were
a little surprised when their efforts led them to the conclusion
that most, but not all of the high priority items for change towards
the objective had to do with the development of the Bank's
employees, and particularly managerial personnel.

Because of the complexity of the issues and the time limits
this case demonstrates an incomplete application of our method
but shows very well its potential for team building at a Senior
Management level, and for clarifying strategic directions and
winning allegiance to them.

The impact of the 'retreat' continues. In discussions a year later
people still refer to ideas and proposals that were raised there.

Summary

This chapter has described a group process in which useful ideas and information can be exchanged and then organised to produce an agreed set of dimensioned variables on which the current state of the organisation may be plotted resulting in a profile of those parts of the organisation relevant to the objective being pursued. This done, questions can be asked about the relative power of the variables to influence the objective and in what way they should be changed. A systematic approach to these questions is set out in Chapter 2.

2 Dealing with blockages

The paths to a desired destination may be many and varied. On close examination, it invariably turns out that some are more easily accessible and easier to negotiate than others. The trick is to find the path, or paths, which reach the goal with least effort. This is the theme of Chapter 2. We shall try (still in the group mode) to identify those variables which, if changed, would powerfully influence the objective and to explore the obstacles to change. This is the beginning of the task of reducing variety and establishing priorities.

An organisation profile

The previous chapter showed how each of the items listed as candidates for inclusion in a plan for beneficial change may be converted into one or more dimensioned variables. A cross placed at a point on the dimension indicates the current state of the variable as agreed by the group, and an arrow extending along the dimension from the cross expresses the view of the group about how the variable would have to be changed if the objective were to be reached. In this as in every step of our general procedure for planning and making changes two processes were involved; one a technical-rational process of deriving variables and dimensions, and allocating crosses and arrows, the other a social process of mutual learning set up in such a way as to aid the development of mutual trust and commitment to a programme of change.

Although we do not recommend it, the technical-rational process could be done without group work at all; it could be entrusted to one person. However, that person would have to seek information from a wide range of sources in order to identify items, and to devise appropriate dimensions. He/ she would also have to rely for the placing of crosses and arrows upon a wide range of (possibly conflicting) opinions and his/her own judgements. None of this seeking would necessarily cause the information givers and opinion staters to be well disposed towards any plan for action. Indeed, as attitude surveyors long since discovered, people who are asked their attitudes and opinions are inclined to assume that changes are being planned in ways which will reflect their wishes and aspirations. If nothing is subsequently changed they could be at least disappointed. At worst they could feel let down believing that their opinions count for nothing. If changes *are* made which do not reflect their opinions, they might feel cheated. Either way they are unlikely to cherish a high sense of responsibility for and commitment to the change and to those who planned it. So, if the process of evolving a plan for change is also to cause a growth of greater commitment and responsibility, the information gathering and the opinion-stating must be integrated with preparation of the plan. This is just as true of the process of variety-reduction, the first steps of which form the subject of this chapter.

To complete the generation of variety all the dimensioned variables must be allocated a cross and an arrow. When this has been completed according to the rules already introduced and exemplified in the previous chapter the result is a 'profile' showing the current state of the organisation in respect of those variables that are considered by the group in the light of their knowledge and experience, to be relevant to the objective. Adding the arrows indicates the judgements of the group concerning the desired direction of change. If the group wishes to record its efforts a chart as illustrated in Figure 2.1 could be produced for future reference. The group will find that it helps to arrange the ends of the scales so that all the arrows are pointing in the same direction as shown.

Variable

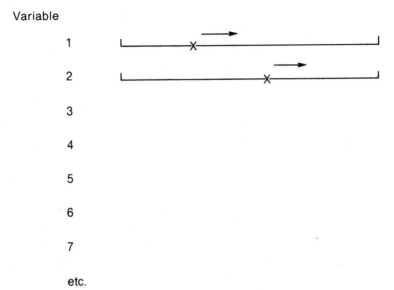

Figure 2.1   Profile of variables and directions of movement

Towards simplicity

What can we do with Figure 2.1? What questions does it raise? How can we work from it towards a simple agreed plan for change? It is possible to treat Figure 2.1 as a list of variables awaiting to be rearranged in order of their priority as levers for achieving a given objective. It might also be thought that the list might in some way be shortened by excluding those variables which looked unpromising. The next of the several steps in our method is designed to order priorities. However, *deletion of apparently unpromising items is not recommended at this stage.* We may need them later for reasons we now briefly discuss.

Organisations as systems

Organisations and their environments are, in our view, usefully considered as systems of interconnected elements, which we have described as (dimensioned) variables. The existence of interconnections implies that changes in any one variable

may cause or be associated with changes in others, directly
and immediately, or through longer chains of consequences.
The most superficial observation reveals that persons who
work in organisations, and especially managers, act as if they
believe that to be the case.

How else is it possible to explain decisions to make, for
example, changes in the management structure of organisations except by assuming that those making the decisions
think that certain consequences will follow that are advantageous to the organisation, or to those who made the decisions,
or both. Take, for example, the most recent of several radical
re-organisations of the National Health Service management
structure which included the creation of the post of general
manager. We may suppose that those recommending the
changes believed that improvements in the coordination of
the work of specialised departments would follow and this
would in turn result, among other things, in the improvement
of service to patients, on some time scale of months or years.
This same may be said of any plan for organisation change
– to introduce new products or processes, new salary structures, new procedures for cost control and so on.

Sometimes actions taken to effect improvements have the
unintended and unanticipated consequence of making things
worse, or at least giving rise to unwelcome and surprising
side effects, all of which are frequently attributed to bad
luck or the unreasonable reactions of those affected by the
changes. To pretend that all the consequences of every change
in every system variable could ever be completely and
accurately anticipated, and that the outcomes would always
remain in the control of the initiator would be to claim god-
like qualities. But we can, by tapping systematically into the
experience of organisational participants and relying less on
guesswork, do much better than we would ordinarily expect.

The reason, therefore, for not deleting any one variable
at this stage is that although it might appear to be unimportant considered in isolation in a one-to-one relationship to
an objective, it might assume greater significance when it
is considered as one among a set of interconnected variables,
and the consequences on other variables of changing it are
traced.

Nothing we have done so far has, however, been directed at establishing the connections between the variables in a systematic way. We have concentrated rather on identifying, defining and measuring all those that seem relevant to our purposes and which are within the power of organisation members to alter. Nor is it the intention of this chapter to explore the nature and magnitude of the connections. This is a difficult and time-consuming task which will be described in detail in the next chapter. The preparation of the profile was an essential preliminary, and the work described in this chapter takes that preparation further.

Potency

Following an earlier example, let us suppose the objective had to do with unit product cost. Suppose also that one of the variables identified was the complexity of the pay system. Let us say that the cross on the variable indicated a current state of high complexity and the arrow pointed towards less complexity. The group can now consider *the extent to which* a reduction in the complexity of the pay system would influence unit cost in the desired direction in the time envisaged. The idea is to judge the *power* of the variable to influence the objective irrespective of any effects it may have on other variables, and express it as a *potency score*. This score represents the magnitude of the slope in the relationship which we discussed in the previous chapter. Quite probably there will be differences of opinion based on knowledge and experience and much discussion might be necessary before agreement is reached to allocate a score. It is just possible that the judgement might be that no amount of reduction of complexity would have any effect on unit cost. In that event the natural impulse is to define the variable as irrelevant and cross it out. For reasons just outlined, this would be unwise and should be strongly resisted, because it would not allow the group to consider, as at a later stage it must, the possibility that a reduction in pay system complexity might work through its effects on other variables to improve unit cost. *The variable must remain in the list even though its individual potency score is zero in relation to the chosen objective.*

A more likely outcome is that the judgement of the group will be that the variable has *some* power to influence the objective. In that event the group has to assign a potency score. The group should decide first whether a small movement along the arrow would have a large effect on the objective or whether a large movement would have a small effect. They must then record their judgement on a scale with 1 at one end and 5 at the other.* We record 1 when the objective is not thought to be *directly* affected by any movement of the variable. If a *very large* change will take place in the objective as a direct result of a *very small* movement of the variable a score of 5 should be assigned, that is, *maximum potency*.

So much for potency and its measurement. When each variable has been assigned a potency score, they must all be considered again, this time to establish the nature and weight of the blocks to movements of the variables in the direction of the arrows. Take the variable 'pay system complexity' and assume, for purposes of illustration, that the group has assigned to it a high potency score, say 4 on the 5 point scale. Now they must address the question 'if the attempt is made to change the variable in the "right" direction, what might block such a change?' The group might easily raise a list of possible blocks and discuss their nature and strength. For example:

	WEAK	AVE	STRONG
• Intrinsic blockages e.g. attitudes			√
• Trade Union resistance		√	
• Shop floor objections			√
• Product variety	√		
• Work flow administration			√

In discussing such a list the detailed nature of the blockage must be fully spelled out and recorded. The record will be needed when detailed planning and implementing of change take place. The detail is needed in order to gauge the cost

---

*This system of numbers is arbitrary. It could be 1–150 if we knew enough about the variables.

and time involved in removing the blockages. These are indications of the strength of the blockage and assist the process of assigning a score for *ease of change*.

As in the case of potency a scale from 1 to 5 should be set up for each variable and an 'ease of change' score assigned. If the group considers that the blocks to changes in the variable are so great that they can only be removed at a cost which would cancel out totally any beneficial effect on the objective then it will assign a score of 1. If there are absolutely no blocks to be found then the score must be 5. In our example where we assumed five possible blocks to the reduction of a pay system complexity, their average propensity to block was rather strong, suggesting a score of 1 or 2 on the ease of change scale.

The outcome of the procedures set out in this chapter is shown in Figure 2.2.

Variable	Potency score A 1–5	Blockage analysis B	Ease of change C 1–5
1 Complexity of pay system	3	Union behaviour Shop floor objections Product variety Work flow admin.	5
2 Attitudes of support staff	5	Pay differentials Craft demarcation Staff turnover	2

and so on for each variable

Figure 2.2 Potency, blockage and ease of change

Remember that Figure 2.2 is concerned only to exhibit the nature of the connection between each variable (considered separately) and the objective. The connections between the variables themselves have yet to be considered in detail. When that is done we may find that some of the items in the blockage analysis column B might turn out to be variables which connect with other variables in ways conducive to positive changes in the objective.

More of that presently. For the moment we can use Figure 2.2 as a step towards a preliminary establishment of priorities among the variables. It will not have escaped notice that a variable with a high potency score and a high ease of change score would have to be placed high on a list of priorities for change. At the bottom of the list would be placed those with both low potency and low ease of change scores. To aid the search for priorities when there are many variables we have found it useful to array all of them in a matrix, positioned according to their scores on potency and ease of change. This is shown in Figure 2.3.

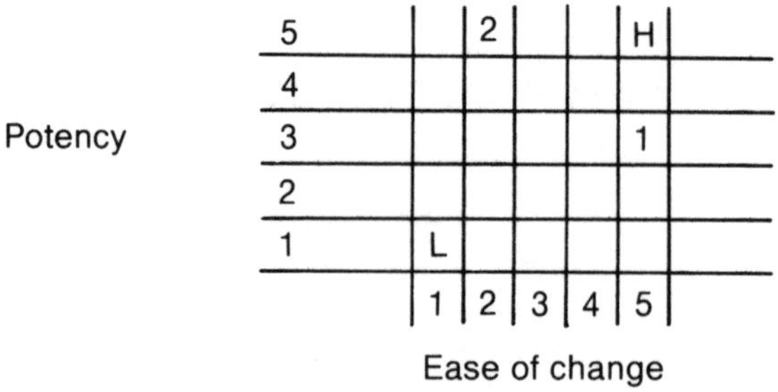

Figure 2.3   Discovering priorities
Note: variable 1 'complexity of pay system' has a potency score of 3 and an ease of change score of 5. Variable 2 'attitudes of support staff' has a potency score of 5 and an ease of change score of 2. Neither will appear as high on a list of priorities as the hypothetical variable H which scores 5 on both potency and ease of change. But both will be higher than the hypothetical variable L which has very low scores on both dimensions

As a further step the group should consider the order in which the variables in the matrix might be placed in a programme of change. Obviously, any variable with a 5/5 score will be placed top of the list – but it is not clear just by examination whether to move along the top row of the matrix looking for powerful variables, or down the right-hand column looking for the ones that are easy to change. The problem is that as one moves along the row the powerful variables become more difficult to change and as one moves down the column the easy-to-change ones become less and less potent. Whether or not this indicates a diagonal movement might rest on a re-consideration by the group of the nature of the blockages in each case. It is possible that the optimum plan might represent a zig-zag course roughly following a diagonal.

However, this cannot be the final plan because the nature of the interdependencies of the variables has not yet been explored. It is entirely possible that a variable with a moderate potency score and which seems moderately difficult to change, will work powerfully on the objective *via* its impact on other variables. If this is so, and in the next chapter we will show some ways of finding out, then the effort needed to remove some of the blockages might be thought worthwhile.

Two outcomes for the group of the steps followed so far are a list of variables arranged in order of priority for change aimed at the objective, and a greatly enhanced and explicit shared understanding of the organisation as a socio-technical-system-in-environment. It cannot be emphasised too strongly again that temptation to cross out the low priority variables is to be resisted. All of them will be needed at further stages of evolving a plan for change. Enhanced understanding of the system and of each other is also a necessary element in that process which is one reason we advise that time should not be skimped in developing it.

A representative group which has come this far could consider reporting to constituents the progress made. Our experience is that to try out interim conclusions in search of a plan for change on those likely to be at the 'receiving end' is a worthwhile exercise. The time and effort devoted to it will be more than repaid at the stage of implementation.

Why do it that way?

One reason for the procedures described earlier in the chapter has already been hinted at. We said that for those who have followed the procedure the outcome should be 'a greatly enhanced and explicitly shared understanding of the organisation as a socio-technical-system-in-environment'. We now have to show what the practical and theoretical point is of understanding the organisation as a socio-technical-system-

in-environment and what the value is of sharing that understanding with others.

> '...any production system requires both a technical
> organisation – equipment and process layout – and a work
> organisation relating to each other those who carry out
> the necessary tasks. The technological demands place limits
> on the type of work organisation possible but a work
> organisation has social and psychological properties of its
> own that are independent of technology. A socio-technical
> system must also satisfy the financial conditions of the
> industry of which it is a part. It must have economic
> validity. It has in fact social, technological and economic
> dimensions all of which are interdependent but all of which
> have independent values of their own'.

> '...inherent in the socio-technical approach is the notion
> that the attainment of optimum conditions in any one
> dimension does not necessarily result in a set of conditions
> optimal for the system as a whole'. (Trist *et al.,* 1968;
> reproduced with permission)

So far we have shown how to draw the outlines of a picture
of any organisational unit seen as a socio-technical-economic
system. In listing the items using the procedures described
in Chapter 1 we drew on the detailed knowledge and experienced judgement of those who know well the technology,
the work organisation, and the economic (labour market and
product market) and technical environment of the unit in
question. In choosing the objective for the whole unit and
not just for a specialised department of it we began the process
of looking for an optimum solution which involved changes
in the total system, and not sub-optimal solutions or changes.
To work with a multi-discipline group as we recommend
means that although the elements of the total picture are
contributed by experienced individuals, the result is a map
of the socio-technical system open to environment influences
which is the property of the whole group.

In Chapter 1 we also showed how *dimensioned variables*
could be derived from the raw items, and how they could

be used to exhibit a profile of the present state of the various elements in the system.

If our procedures had not been designed expressly for a practical purpose; if all we had wished to do was to exhibit a profile of the present state of the total system we would have made our objective a dimensioned variable and added it to the list, placed a cross on it, and removed the arrows from all the dimensions. That would then be a static picture of the state of the system elements at a given date. The procedure from then on would have been to ask 'what would happen if' questions, that is, questions about what would happen to the profile of the total system-in-environment if some variables started to or were made to vary along their dimensions. How would the whole new profile look at a later time? Shifts on some variables will occur when conditions in environments change which are outside the control of those within the boundaries of the system, such as, for example, the behaviour of customers and competitors, change in employee attitudes because of labour market shifts, or alterations in Trade Union policy. Or they may be varied by those with authority within the boundaries of the system, perhaps with the intention of shifting some of the environmental variables, for example, changes in pricing policy, or product range, or sales organisation, in order to influence the behaviour of customers and competitors; and changes in wage structures or dispute procedures to influence the policies and behaviour of unions.

There is certainly the promise of practical benefits to be gained by constructing such profiles and working out complex strategies from the answers to 'what would happen if' questions. It is also possible, having by this means elucidated the pattern of interdependencies between the variables, to choose that variable which is to be nominated as an objective, so that movements along the other variables can be planned, with the purpose of influencing the objective in directions thought to be desirable. In Chapter 5 we shall show in detail how objectives can be chosen in this way and in Chapter 3 how the interdependencies can be mapped by the 'what happens if' procedure.

Our purpose in this chapter was more limited. We took

each dimensioned variable separately, and related it separately to the chosen objective in terms of its potency and the ease of changing it. We were not measuring general potency (indeed it is difficult to imagine such a thing) nor potency in relation to the system of variables as a whole, but only potency in relation to the variable chosen as the objective. This enabled us to have a first shot at simplifying matters while still holding on to all the dimensioned variables as parts of a system to be explored and turned to practical use in further stages of the procedure. We discovered as a result which variables show promise as levers to move the system in ways which will achieve the objectives, that is, those on the top right-hand corner of the matrix and those which *in terms of the chosen objective* show less promise. But we have not yet begun in earnest to explore the inter-dependencies between the dimensioned variables in any detail and until we have done so, we cannot finish our plan making.

We are convinced that the individuals who have taken part in the procedures described so far will, whether fully conscious of it or not, have begun to understand their organisation as a socio-technical, etc. system; realising that the list of dimensioned variables which emerged includes social, technical, psychological and economic ones and that those can be usefully considered as system elements with an equal claim for consideration, at least to the point that changes in them are likely to result in more or less powerful, measured effects on a valued objective. At most there could be a realisation of the great potentialities of the concepts and procedures as tools for making plans, predicting the outcome of implementing them, and learning from having done it.

If our assumptions as to social process are right these new insights arising from and including the use of practical procedures will be shared by the members of the group and will affect the way they relate to each other in their work, as well as the way they think about how to solve problems.

Difficulties

Group members may continue to find difficulty in working

outside their accustomed professional frames of reference or in unfamiliar conceptual and experimental territory. They might also exhibit initial puzzlement as to whether the advantages of doing it outweigh the mental effort and time required. In the early stages of our procedure these two can add up to formidable psychological barriers to effective co-operation. These should have begun to ease when the process of variety reduction starts as described in the present chapter.

Difficulties during the assignment of potency and ease of change scores can obviously arise because of conflicting opinions and viewpoints. The extent to which the members of the group share a common conception of the nature of the system they work in is likely to increase markedly through the stages of item-listing and drawing dimensioned variables, but it will represent far less than complete consensus by the time the group begins to place crosses and arrows. To avoid argument, some group members might be inclined to defer to the specialist in whose domain a particular variable is located in the expectation that they will defer to his/her variables in his/her domain. For example – financial controller = knowledge about cash flows, personnel manager = knowledge about training. This is unhelpful. The financial controller may indeed be supremely competent in methods of tracing and recording cash flows. He will also have views about what the record means for some aspects of the economic health of the organisation. He/she might not have considered seriously the kinds of questions which are raised when potency and ease of change scores are being considered. For example, the group might be ready to go along with the opinion of the specialist that an increase in positive cash flow might have beneficial effects. Yet, some members might have reason and fact in their support when questioning his/her view about potency and ease of change. One thinks, for example, of the sales manager with his special knowledge of the order book and the purchasing manager who is sensitive to price changes among suppliers, and so on. The financial controller's opinions may be no more reliable on these matters than anybody else's. The same could apply equally of course to the personnel manager whose thoughts about the power of some variables representing training to influence unit product cost may be less than completely thought through, and based on limited knowledge.

It would be equally foolish, of course, to ignore the specialist if it turns out that his opinion is backed by more powerful logic and evidence than other members of the group as they become engrossed in the process of plotting the state of the system by their crosses and arrows and as they map the system's potential for changing the objective by the way they assign the scores for potency and ease of change.

Some of the same kinds of difficulties might arise when various paths through the 5 × 5 matrix are being plotted as early attempts to delineate possible planned sequences of change are made.

By this stage, we believe, the group will have developed a more open style, so that everyone's views (while respected) are open to challenge.

Summary

This chapter has shown how systematic attention can be given to the power of each variable, taken separately, to influence an objective and how relative power can be indicated by position on a scale. A score can also be assigned to each variable to indicate the strength of the obstacles that lie in the path of change. This scoring has two effects. The first is to put the variables in rough order of priority for changing, reducing dramatically the necessary variety generated by Step 1; and the second is to add to the group's commitment to support the emerging plan for change. In the next chapter we shall show how variety can be further reduced and commitment further enhanced.

Reference

TRIST, E. L. *et al., Organisational Choice,* Tavistock, London, 1968

3   Planning for action

Systems are not defined by lists of discrete variables such as have been dealt with so far. They are characterised essentially by the connections of imputed causation between variables. It is one thing to ask about the relative power of variables taken separately to influence an objective, it is another to consider the connections between the variables themselves and the relationships of those connections to the objective. The least effort principle demands that we look for the variables which, if changed, would set off the most powerful chain reactions towards the objective. This is the next step in the procedure and the subject of this chapter.

So far we have followed the steps necessary to construct a 'profile' representing the present state of the organisational unit under consideration. The shape of the profile was determined by placing a cross on each dimensioned variable according to the considered judgement of the group. An arrow originating at the cross indicated the opinion of the group as to the direction of movement along each variable that was necessary to achieve the objective.

We used the profile to raise questions about the power of each variable to influence the objective and the answers to them enabled us to assign a 'potency' score for each. Blockages in the path of change were then identified and used to arrive at an 'ease of change' score for each variable. It was then possible to identify some variables for priority treatment and to try some paths through the 5 × 5 matrix looking at the sequences of change which seemed likely to give the

best results with the least effort. We also looked in a preliminary way at the relationships of cause and effect connecting each variable to the others as a preparation for the work
of this chapter.

We are ready now to map out in detail all the interconnections between the variables. The purpose of doing so
is to identify those variables which if changed in the direction
indicated by the arrows on the profile would have the maximum positive effect on the others in causing them also to
move in the direction indicated by the arrow.

For example, it is not too difficult to envisage our group
judging that to move along a dimensioned variable from a
position where the training of supervisors is relatively
informal to a position where more formality is introduced,
would start a positive move along a dimension representing
supervisory attitudes of cooperation. In its turn this might
be judged to cause a positive movement along a number
of dimensions representing the cost and quality of output.
Of course it could well be that a positive movement along
one dimension could cause a negative movement along
another or indeeed could have no effect at all.

A convenient and useful way to present the results of the
judgements of the group as to the nature and magnitude
of the chains of cause and effect connecting all the variables
is the cross-impact matrix.

Cross-impact analysis and the matrix

The object of cross-impact analysis is to provide a means
for considering the systemic consequences of any particular
set of actions. We start by looking at each dimensioned
variable in turn and asking what impact the desired change
on this variable would have upon each of the other dimensioned variables which have been included in the analysis,
which means the complete list produced by the procedure
followed in Chapter 1. Admittedly cross-impact analysis does
not show how the system would react if several variables
were changed simultaneously but it is a great improvement
on the commonly practised approach in which only the

relationships between isolated pairs of variables are considered. Although cross-impact analysis does not enable us to see how simultaneous action on two or more dimensions would actually modify the relationships between other variables taken singly or severally, it does allow us to use the inter-relationships between variables as we have plotted them to further our overall purposes in planning and making changes.

In particular we can look for reactions in other variables which positively reinforce actions we propose to take and we can discover and seek to avoid reactions which undermine our plans. In order to do this we have to construct a matrix of impacts which records the expected interactions among the variables within the system. This matrix is produced by considering each dimensioned variable in turn and examining the impact which the desired change in it would have upon each of the other dimensions. As we shall see, the precision which can be achieved in the estimation of the impacts may vary greatly according to the complexity of the system and our confidence in our knowledge of it. This is not crucial – we can only work at a level of accuracy which corresponds to the quality and quantity of the information available and our confidence in the reliability of our judgements. At worst we may only be able to guess at the direction of the impact – that is, whether it is positive or negative in the light of our purposes. Even in these circumstances the matrix will provide useful guidance as to courses of action.

More commonly, as we have found, it will be possible to discern not only the direction but also the magnitude of the impacts which we have to consider. In most applications of this procedure we have found it to be sufficient to discriminate between those impacts which are relatively minor and those which are major movements along the dimensions. The description of the procedure which follows assumes this level of discrimination. Where much finer judgements can be made about the effects of change these can be incorporated in the analysis, but the reliability of the information included is more important than the fineness of detail.

The cross-impact matrix has as many columns and rows as there are variables to be considered. Each row when complete will contain information concerning the impact of a

particular variable on all the other variables. It is completed
by repeatedly asking how the change in the row variable
will impact upon the successive column variables – and
recording for each pairing the 'score' which represents the
magnitude and direction of the impact. Thus, if we were
using a scoring system with + and − representing direction
and 1 and 10 representing small and large magnitude, as
shown in Figure 3.1, the rows would be filled with a string
of scores such as +1 +10 −1 0 0 −1 0 0 +1... and
so on (where 0 indicates no impact). That is, nothing happens
scores 0, small change in desired direction scores +1, large
change in desired direction scores +10, small change in
undesirable direction scores −1, large change in undesirable
direction scores −10. We recommend that as the group considers each pair of variables the members not only agree
on a 'score' but they also record the nature of the impact,
that is, they write a short summary of the reason why they
have allocated the score. To do this in a disciplined way
will certainly ensure that scores are not allocated without
due thought and exchange of experience, but just as
importantly it provides information of great value when at
a later stage a plan is worked out in detail for making changes
in an ordered sequence which will modify the system to meet
the objective in the time scale envisaged.

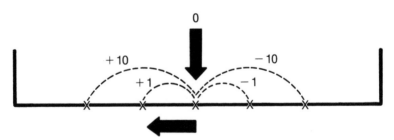

Figure 3.1   Scoring system showing five possibilities

To illustrate using an example already cited: suppose that
dimensioned variable 1 is the degree of formality of training
of supervisors, and that the arrow is indicating greater
formality. We are considering the impact of a move towards

greater formality in this training on variable 2 which depicts supervisory attitudes to management; ranging from low to high cooperation. We might decide that such a move would have a powerful positive effect on variable 2 (that is, supervisory attitudes would become considerably more cooperative as a result) and therefore to allocate a score of $+10$. Our reasoning for this is that by the act of introducing more formal training managers are showing interest in helping supervisors with their problems, which will induce them to change their attitudes. This reason should be recorded. A form for keeping such records is shown in Figure 3.2.

Factors	Nature of impact	Degree of impact
–and–		-10 1 0 1 $10+$
–and–		-10 1 0 1 $10+$
–and–		-10 1 0 1 $10+$
–and–		-10 1 0 1 $10+$
–and–		-10 1 0 1 $10+$
–and–		-10 1 0 1 $10+$
–and–		-10 1 0 1 $10+$
–and–		-10 1 0 1 $10+$
–and–		-10 1 0 1 $10+$

Figure 3.2   Record of comments in developing cross-impact matrix

This is a lengthy task where, as can be the case, 50 or more variables are involved but there is no avoiding it if the analysis of the systemic effects of change is to be carried out as it must. It is tempting to try to save time by completing only half of the matrix, assuming that the impact of variable 1 on 3 is the same as the impact of variable 3 on 1. A moment's reflection reveals that this could never be so if we consider the actual events which comprise the impact.

These events may be represented by the same score in the matrix but this should not be allowed to disguise the fact that they are nonetheless different and that it is necessary to discover both.

The procedure for constructing the cross-impact matrix is very simple and relatively straightforward if a few basic conditions are observed. First it must be remembered that the matrix is supposed to record the effects of change within the system. It is therefore important that we consider how a change in one variable will influence the state of another. Moreover we are interested in the effects of a *particular* change in each variable – that which we would plan to carry out in order to achieve our objective. It is surprisingly easy to fall into the trap of considering and recording some general interaction which would follow the given change. For example, one group of managers were working on a matrix which included the dimension 'raw material prices'. After a while the question to which they addressed themselves each time the impact of a change in raw material prices was considered was 'do raw material prices have any impact on *yyy*?'. The specific question on which they should have focused was 'will our actions to reduce raw material prices have any impact on *yyy*?'. The expected impacts of the general and the specific are often very dissimilar and groups should always be alert for this mistake.

Secondly it is most important that the matrix represents the inevitable automatic consequences of the various proposed changes. The matrix must be the best estimate of how things will change in response to actions on the variables. It is therefore important to avoid the tendency to argue that a particular change would 'make it easier to do *x*' and thus have a positive impact upon it. This is not what is meant; the impact must be in the form of an observable movement along the defined dimensions.

The third important condition for a meaningful analysis is that the time scale should be consistent within the matrix and appropriate to the nature of the system under consideration. The consistency must be maintained within the matrix so that we have a common basis for comparison of the different impacts. If we were to carry out the analysis without referring in every case to the time period within which any effects had to occur, we might end up with some which were manifest in a few months whereas others were expected to take decades. The decision as to which particular time scale to adopt may have to be arbitrary although in most cases it is not difficult to establish an agreed planning horizon, indeed the initial objective is likely to include one. It is even possible to consider repeating the analysis for each of two or three different time scales where it is felt that significant differences may be revealed which could be useful in deciding between short and long term strategies possibly leading to a revision of the original time scale.

A completed matrix would look like Figure 3.3.

Dimensioned
variable
Nos   Totals

	2	4	6	8	9	11	12	17	18	19	+	−
2		10	10	0	−1	1	0	1	0	0	22	1
4	10		10	0	10	1	0	10	0	0	41	0
6	10	10		0	0	1	1	1	0	0	23	0
8	10	10	1		1	1	10	10	−1	0	43	1
9	−1	−10	0	0		10	1	1	−1	0	12	12
11	1	0	1	0	0		1	10	0	0	13	0
12	0	0	0	0	0	0		1	−1	0	1	1
17	−1	0	0	0	0	1	−1		0	0	1	2
18	0	0	−1	−10	0	0	−10	1		10	11	21
19	0	0	0	0	0	0	0	0	0		0	0
Totals +	31	30	22	0	11	15	13	35	0	10		
−	2	10	1	10	1	0	11	0	3	0		

Figure 3.3   Example of completed matrix
Note: the variables 2, 4, 6, 8, 9, 11, 12, 17, 18, 19 have all been chosen from a longer list for purposes of illustration

Learning from the matrix

There is a lot to be learned from such a matrix, but first it is necessary to summarise some of the information which it contains. First, go along each row in turn and add all the positive scores together. Then go down the columns and do the same. Now add the negative scores as well to give a total for each row and column. The result is exemplified already in Figure 3.3. We can readily discover from these scores the degree of consistency which exists among the proposed changes of the variables. The lower the negative score for the whole matrix the more consistent the set of changes would be. Negative scores indicate a conflict between the desired change in one variable and some other. The fact that these have been revealed in the matrix is one of the major justifications for its use. Where these negative consequences of particular changes are either very large or numerous, or worse still both, it may be necessary to abandon any thought of proceeding with those changes.

Case study 4   The perils of neglecting system connections

Food processing is a highly competitive business, compelling managers to seek ways of reducing costs and providing a high standard of quality and service to customers, that is, wholesalers and retailers.

Charcutes, a large company with several factories, is in business to transform dead pigs into bacon, sausages, pork pies and such delicacies. The pigs are bred and reared under contract by farmers all over Britain who follow procedures devised by experts employed by the company. To ensure consistent body weight, plumpness, shape and so on the live pigs, having reached the appropriate point in their physical growth and development, are despatched in trucks to the factory, and assembled in pens ready to await slaughter. The logistics of this operation are complicated. Things have to be organised in such a way that exactly the right number of pigs are transported to, and assembled in the pens each day to balance with the slaughtering, processing, cold storage and delivery operations. The senior managers of the company were looking for ways of reducing costs to a competitive level and to ensure reliable deliveries while maintaining quality. Four possibilities were:

1   To reduce the high costs of cold storage and transport costs.

2   To improve the type of animal so as to reduce waste in processing, and produce products of high quality.

3   To mechanise the processing operation.

4   To reduce product variety.

Each of these concerns, as might be expected, fitted quite neatly into the structure of management specialisms. So the distribution department was asked to come up with some ideas (showing possible costs and benefits) under item 1; the genetics and animal husbandry experts at head office were directed to item 2, manufacturing management to item 3, and the sales and marketing department to item 4. The departments worked separately, and reported separately to top management.

It was not thought feasible to cut product variety, partly because of the nature of the beast (literally) and partly because of market demand. The costs of developing new technology far outweighed the short to medium term benefits, so the idea of mechanisation was shelved. However, the people looking at pig 'design' and cold storage came up with some attractive proposals. It was shown that great savings would accrue if the massive cold stores, filled as they were with products awaiting orders from customers, were closed down and replaced by small freezers on the customers' (retailers) premises (on hire from Charcutes) to which finished products could be delivered daily fresh off the end of the line in the existing refrigerated trucks. At the input end the new pig would be delivered, easier to cut-up, making less waste, resulting in better bacon, pies, and sausages, at competitive prices. It was decided to make the changes as recommended. This disguised version of a true story exhibits not untypical managerial behaviour.

The management was shattered, when, shortly after the replacement of the cold storage buildings and the arrival of the new pig, the slaughtermen went out on wildcat strike, led by a militant shop steward of a powerful union who belonged to an immigrant minority well represented in the slaughterhouse. The strike was a near disaster for the company economically. The production and rearing of pigs cannot be suddenly stopped and started again, and contracts have to be honoured (and 'stored' pigs tend to deteriorate and become unsuitable for transformation into quality products). At the output end the plant had no buffer between the production process and the market.

The questions that had *not* been addressed at the outset were questions apposite to the connection between the technical and market variables and the labour market and industrial relations variables. In the 'inquest' on the strike, the following facts came to light.

1   Slaughterers had been for some time so difficult to come by that the personnel department spent a lot of money on recruiting and training immigrants. Turnover was high.

2   The slaughterers were using their labour market power to press for pay increases which would erode the differentials with less well-organised, less scarce, less numerous non-immigrant groups.

3   The foremen were a particular example. To leave themselves free to press their own claims they had left the union to which the slaughterers also belonged, and started one of their own. The slaughterers' union was in dispute with the management over this issue at the time the new technical changes were being made, with the official support of their head office.

4   The leader of the foremen's breakaway was the supervisor in the department where the shop steward worked.

5   The shop steward was an aggressive, impulsive person.

6   The strike was precipitated when the shop steward threatened to close the plant down, insisting that either the foreman who organised the breakaway be sacked, or he would take the slaughterers out, which he did.

The point is that no-one in management ever intended the strike to happen but the re-organisation increased sharply the bargaining power of the shop steward, and the defensive acts of the foreman provided the occasion to exercise it.

Had the pursuit of improved efficiency been conducted so that the facts and the connections came to light *before* action, rather than at the 'inquest' afterwards, possible obstacles could have been jointly identified and opportunities to surmount them jointly explored. Our method allows that to be systematically done.

Here too we can see the reason for including as many variables in the analysis as time and knowledge allow because the negative impacts may occur on variables which would not themselves be seen as likely levers for change. This is why in Chapter 2 we insisted that no variables be struck out. If they were excluded from the analysis the possibility that they might be adversely affected by other changes could not be investigated. Even if no change is desired or envisaged in a particular variable it should be included as a passive element in the matrix. A passive element is one of which we only ask how changes in other variables impact upon it, we do not ask what impact it will have on them. In this way some unexpected problems can be brought to light and the possibility of avoiding them can be explored.

The positive scores in the matrix indicate the degree of congruence which the various changes have with one another. Obviously, the higher the positive scores the more the changes will tend to reinforce one another. The fact that the matrix has been very carefully completed to reflect the automatic responses among variables allows us to make further use of these positive relationships. Any positive element in the matrix offers us the possibility of reducing the number of variables on which we have to act in order to carry through the set of changes. The presence of several positive elements opens up the possibility of 'chaining' the impacts in such a way that only a very small proportion of the variables may have to be changed by direct action on our part. If we choose the right starting point the majority of the changes may come about as a result of the chain reaction in the system. This will save considerable effort and resources which would otherwise have been expended on the changes on variables which are brought about by the impacts.

It may help to follow the analysis of a matrix using a particular example like that shown in Figure 3.4.

	1	2	3	4	5	6	7	8	9	10		
1		10	0	0	-1	1	10	1	0	0	21	-1
2	0		0	10	0	1	0	0	0	1	12	0
3	-10	1		1	0	0	-10	1	1	0	4	-20
4	0	1	0		0	1	0	0	1	0	3	0
5	10	0	10	10		1	0	0	10	1	42	0
6	1	0	0	10	0		1	10	0	1	23	0
7	-10	0	0	0	10	1		10	-1	0	21	-11
8	1	0	10	10	0	1	10		0	1	33	0
9	0	0	0	1	1	10	0	1		0	13	0
10	-1	0	0	-1	10	0	-1	0	0		10	3

Figure 3.4   Matrix analysis

The first concern in analysing the matrix is to be alert
to the potential difficulties and dangers which lie in the
changes being considered. These are indicated by the negative
scores in the matrix, each of which should be reviewed to
determine whether the damage which it represents to the
system can be restricted, repaired or counteracted. The major
negatives like those resulting from dimensions 3 and 7 will,
of course, attract our attention first since we have already
judged them to be a serious threat to one of the variables
in which we are interested. As a result of this first inspection
of the matrix we may wish to exclude dimensions like 3 from
consideration as levers for change because of their negative
effects upon the system as a whole.

Our next concern is to discover which subset of the variables which we have included offers the greatest opportunity
for moving towards the objective. We do this by looking
at the positive total for each of the rows in the matrix. The
higher this 'score', the greater the beneficial effect of changing
the variable in the way decided upon at stage two of the
procedure. A high score like that for dimensions 5 and 8
indicates that the variable will cause many other variables
to be changed in ways which move the system towards the

objective. Where the impact of one variable upon another is judged to be substantial it may be unnecessary to take any further action to reach the desired state in that second variable. Herein lies the prime benefit of the cross-impact analysis: *by judicious selection of those variables with impacts on others within the system we may be able to complete all the necessary changes by acting on a small proportion of the total number of variables involved.*

Obviously the potential for this saving in time and effort is determined by the connectedness of the system being tackled. A highly connected system will have very few zero scores in the matrix of impacts while a relatively disconnected system will have a large number of zeros in the matrix.

Case study 5   Actual example of cross-impact analysis

In the case of the mass production plant discussed earlier, it took another day at a later date for the group to complete its analysis. The resulting matrix shown as Figure 3.5 revealed a relatively independent set of variables. Three or four variables did stand out among the others in the range of their impacts upon the system being considered. Foremost among these was one which was concerned with shift payment arrangements. If these could be changed in the desired direction then no fewer than twenty of the fifty identified variables would have been positively affected by its direct impacts and a further sixteen would have been affected by its indirect, secondary, impacts. We look now at the following list of variables.

1   Component grades

2   Stock rotation

3   Rough stock input

4   Faulty components

5   Faulty builds

6   One shift operation

7   Misc. components

8   EP components

9   Cost of inventory

10   Breakdowns — electrical

11   Breakdowns — mechanical

12   New electronics

13   Organisation of maintenance

14   Supply of electrical expertise

15   Supply of electronic expertise

16   Complexity of batch size

17   Special batch

18   Non-standard components

19   Interdependence of machines

20   Machine capability

21   Non-static labour force

22   Late shift labour inefficiency

23   Custom & practice

24   Operator cooperation

25   Quality of labour

26   Stewards

27   Supervisory involvement in service area

28   Service to line — PPC

29   Service to line — maintenance

30   Service to line — engineering

31   Service to line — quality control

32   Space

33   Demarcation

34   Shop steward time off job

35   Training operators

36   Skill training off job

37   Training induction

38   Informing supervisor

39   Supervisor informing operator

40   Ethnic complexity

41   Sabotage

42   Supervisor training

43   Supervisor's content

44   Supervisors (local)

45   Reward for shift system

46   Noise

47   Heat

48   Lighting

49   Line speed

50   Management team

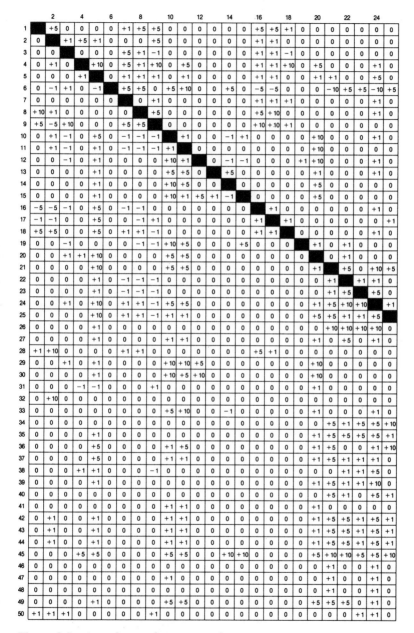

Figure 3.5 Actual cross-impact matrix

26		28		30		32		34		36		38		40		42		44		46		48		50		
0	+1	+5	0	0	0	+1	0	0	0	0	0	0	+1	0	0	0	0	0	0	0	0	0	0	+1	+35	−0
0	+1	+10	0	0	+1	+5	0	0	0	0	0	0	+1	0	0	0	0	0	0	0	0	0	0	+1	+32	−0
0	+1	+1	0	0	0	−1	0	0	0	0	0	0	0	0	0	0	0	0	0	0	0	0	0	+1	+11	−3
0	+5	+1	+5	+1	+5	+1	0	0	0	0	0	0	+1	0	0	0	0	0	0	0	0	0	0	+5	+74	−0
0	0	0	+1	+1	+5	0	0	0	0	0	0	0	+1	0	−1	0	0	0	0	0	0	0	0	+1	+22	−1
−10	+1	+1	+5	0	0	−1	0	+1	0	0	0	+1	0	0	+1	0	0	0	0	0	−1	0	0	0	+56	−44
0	+1	+1	0	0	+1	+1	0	0	0	0	0	0	0	0	0	0	0	0	0	0	−1	0	0	+1	+9	−1
0	+5	+5	0	0	+1	−1	0	0	0	0	0	0	0	0	0	0	0	0	0	0	0	0	0	+5	+47	−1
0	+1	+1	+1	0	0	−10	0	0	0	0	0	0	0	0	0	0	0	0	0	0	0	0	0	−1	+49	−16
0	+10	0	+5	0	0	0	0	0	0	0	0	0	+1	0	+1	+1	0	0	0	0	−1	0	0	+1	+38	−6
0	+5	0	+5	+10	0	0	0	0	0	0	0	0	0	0	0	0	0	0	0	0	0	0	0	+1	+34	−4
0	+5	0	+5	+1	0	−1	0	0	0	0	0	0	+1	0	−1	+1	0	0	0	0	0	0	0	+1	+37	−5
0	+5	0	+10	+1	0	0	0	0	0	0	0	0	+1	0	+1	+1	0	0	0	0	0	0	0	+1	+36	−0
0	+5	0	+10	+1	0	0	0	0	0	0	0	0	+1	0	0	0	0	0	0	0	0	0	0	0	+38	−0
0	+1	0	+10	+1	0	0	0	0	0	0	0	0	+1	0	+1	0	0	0	0	0	0	0	0	0	+37	−1
0	+1	+5	0	0	+5	−1	0	0	0	0	0	0	0	0	0	0	0	0	0	0	0	0	0	0	+18	−14
0	+1	+1	0	0	+1	0	0	0	0	0	0	0	0	0	0	0	0	0	0	0	0	0	0	0	+12	−3
0	0	+1	0	0	+1	+1	0	0	0	0	0	0	0	0	0	0	0	0	0	0	0	0	0	0	+23	−1
0	0	0	+5	+5	0	−10	0	0	0	0	0	0	+1	0	0	+1	0	0	0	0	0	0	0	+1	+22	−13
0	+1	0	+1	+1	+5	0	0	0	0	0	0	0	+1	0	0	0	0	0	0	0	0	0	0	+1	+33	−0
+1	+5	+1	+1	+1	+1	0	0	+1	0	+1	0	+1	+1	+5	0	0	0	0	0	0	0	0	0	+1	+61	−0
+1	+1	0	0	0	0	0	0	+1	0	0	0	+1	0	0	0	0	0	0	0	0	0	0	0	0	+8	−3
+1	0	0	0	0	0	0	0	+1	0	0	0	0	0	0	0	0	0	0	0	0	0	0	0	0	+12	−3
+5	+1	0	+5	+1	+1	0	0	+5	0	0	0	+10	0	+5	0	0	0	0	0	0	0	0	0	+1	+81	−1
+1	0	0	+1	0	+1	0	0	+1	0	0	0	+1	0	+1	0	0	0	0	0	0	0	0	0	0	+37	−1
■	0	0	0	0	0	0	0	+10	0	0	0	+10	0	+1	0	0	0	0	0	0	0	0	0	0	+62	−0
0	■	−5	−1	−1	0	0	0	0	0	0	0	+1	0	0	0	0	0	0	0	0	0	0	0	+1	+11	−7
0	+5	■	0	0	0	0	0	0	0	0	0	0	0	0	0	0	0	0	0	0	0	0	0	+1	+25	−0
0	+5	−1	■	+5	0	0	0	0	0	0	0	+1	0	0	+1	0	0	0	0	0	0	0	0	+5	+55	−1
0	+1	0	+10	■	0	0	0	0	0	0	0	+1	0	0	+1	0	0	0	0	0	0	0	0	+5	+53	−0
0	+1	0	0	−1	■	0	0	0	0	0	0	0	0	0	0	0	0	0	0	0	0	0	0	+10	+13	−4
0	0	+5	0	0	0	■	0	0	0	0	0	0	0	0	0	0	0	0	0	0	0	0	0	0	+15	−0
0	+1	0	+10	0	0	0	■	0	0	0	0	0	0	0	0	0	0	0	+1	+1	+1	0	+5		+36	−1
−5	0	0	0	0	0	0	0	■	0	0	0	+1	+1	0	0	0	0	0	0	0	0	0	0	+1	+29	−5
−1	0	0	0	0	0	0	0	+1	■	+1	0	0	+1	0	+1	0	0	0	0	0	0	0	0	0	+27	−1
0	0	0	0	0	0	0	0	0	■	0	0	+1	0	+1	+1	0	0	0	0	0	0	0	0	0	+27	−0
−1	0	0	0	+1	0	0	+5	0	0	■	0	+10	+1	+1	0	0	0	0	0	0	0	0	0	+5	+37	−2
+1	0	0	0	0	0	0	0	+1	0	0	■	+10	0	0	0	0	0	0	0	0	0	0	0	+1	+19	−0
+1	+1	0	0	0	0	0	0	0	0	+1	0	■	0	+1	0	0	0	0	0	0	0	0	0	0	+24	−0
+1	0	0	0	0	0	0	0	0	0	0	+1	■	0	0	0	0	0	0	0	0	0	0	0	0	+14	−0
0	0	0	0	0	0	0	0	0	0	0	0	0	■	0	0	0	0	0	0	0	0	0	0	0	+3	−0
0	0	0	+1	+1	0	0	0	0	0	0	0	+1	0	■	0	+1	0	0	0	0	0	0	0	+1	+26	−0
0	0	0	+1	+1	0	0	0	0	0	0	0	+1	0	0	+1	■	0	0	0	0	0	0	0	+1	+27	−0
0	0	0	+1	+1	0	0	0	0	0	0	0	+1	0	0	+1	0	■	0	0	0	0	0	0	+1	+25	−0
+5	+5	+5	+10	0	+5	0	+10	0	0	+10	0	0	0	0	0	0	0	■	0	0	0	0	0	+5	+140	−0
+1	0	0	0	0	0	0	+1	0	0	0	0	0	0	0	0	0	0	0	■	0	0	0	0	0	+4	−0
+1	0	0	0	0	0	0	0	0	0	0	0	0	0	0	0	0	0	0	0	■	0	0	0	0	+3	−0
+1	0	0	0	0	0	0	0	0	0	0	0	0	0	0	0	0	0	0	0	0	■	0	0	0	+2	−0
+1	+1	+1	+1	0	0	0	0	0	0	0	0	0	0	0	0	0	0	0	0	0	0	■	0	0	+31	−0
0	+1	+1	+1	+1	+1	0	0	0	0	0	0	+5	+5	0	0	0	0	0	0	0	0	0	0	■	+21	−0

Given a reasonable level of connectedness, the next task is to find the smallest set of variables which leads, via its impacts, to the positive movement of all the variables. This is a simple task although with large matrices it can be time-consuming. Starting with the variable with the highest positive row total (no. 5 in Figure 3.4), which will always be included in the set, list those variables which it impacts upon.

		1	2	3	4	5	6	7	8	9	10
(a)	5:	10	0	10	10	×	1	0	0	10	1

Then inspect the impacts of the second highest scoring variable (no. 8 here); if these include some which were not impacted by the first variable then this second variable should be added to the set. If, however, they include no additional variables then this second variable is not included in the set because we are seeking the smallest set consistent with covering the whole system. Add the impacts of 5 and 8.

		1	2	3	4	5	6	7	8	9	10
(b)	5+8:	11	0	20	20	0	2	10	×	10	2

This process of inspection and comparison should continue until all the variables have been brought in by the impact of others, unless of course they have been included in the set itself. If the system is highly connected the set will be made up of a small number of variables and we will be able to proceed to implement the changes desired with much less demand upon resources than would have been required if our approach had not been informed by this analysis.

In our example variables 6 and 7 are omitted from the set as they add no other variables to the impacts. So the next variable to be included is variable no. 1 which gives the following amalgamated row.

		1	2	3	4	5	6	7	8	9	10
(c)	5+8+1:	11	10	20	20	0 −1	3	20	1	10	2

Notice that all variables are now included in the impacts

although nos. 6 and 10 are only affected in a minor way. No. 6 can be impacted quite strongly by variables 9 and 10. 10 has negative effects whereas 9 has none so 9 should be added to the set.

		1	2	3	4	5	6	7	8	9	10
(d)	$5+8+1+9$:	11	10	20	21	$+1$	13	20	$+1$	10	2
						-1			-1		

Even in relatively unconnected systems, where the set of 'levers' is large in relation to the total number of variables considered, there will be some saving of effort where the cross-impact analysis brings to light advantageous impacts.

We can now select the variable(s) which offer the greatest impact on the system for possible inclusion in our plans for change. The decision which dimensions to choose can be aided by the use of the potency estimates which we produced earlier. These can be used to weight the impacts' scores within the matrix so that impacts on more potent dimensions 'count' for more in the row totals. This is simply achieved by multiplying each column score by the potency value for the appropriate variable.

In making this choice we should also be aware of the blockage score of the variables so that we can choose the paths of least resistance wherever that coincides with worthwhile chains of impact. It may, however, be necessary to contemplate attempting a highly resistant dimension in order to gain significant overall movement within the system. This procedure does not absolve the decision maker from the difficulties of choosing among competing actions but it does lay out the bases for that choice with a level of clarity rarely achieved in the normal course of decision making.

This may be as far as we can go with the analysis of the matrix if we cannot be confident of the stability of the relationships recorded beyond the initial time scale which we established for the analysis. We may have chosen a very long time scale in the first instance and therefore any events beyond that period would be likely to be difficult to predict. Or we may be attempting to change a system about which we know so little that the uncertainty associated with even quite short time periods would deter extended analysis. In many cases, however, it is possible to have sufficient confidence in the stability of the system as represented by the matrix to allow some further stages in the analysis.

Where this is the case we can follow the logic of the matrix to discover the full extent of the chains of impact which are embedded within it. We have already discovered those dimensions which are most useful in causing others to move in directions desirable to us. When we cause them to change we can expect them to cause other variables to change in the ways we have predicted, but these other variables are themselves likely to have some impact both among themselves and on yet other variables. We can discover what these impacts are by inspecting the appropriate rows of the matrix. These will be what we might call the second-order effects of the changes with which we began. They can be expected to occur as a result of the initial changes but only after a time lag of up to twice the chosen time scale.

The limit to the number of iterations of this sort that can be analysed will be determined either by the increasing uncertainty associated with ever lengthening time scales or by the exhaustion of fruitful chains within the matrix. The lower the general level of scoring within the matrix the sooner it will become exhausted in this way.

Analysis of these chains of interaction over time offers further possibilities for the decision maker to discern the patterns of initial change which are most advantageous as their effects ramify through the system. The choices made after this stage of analysis may be quite different from those which would have been made on the basis of the first-order impacts alone. This can happen where one or two variables have high initial impacts which are nonetheless associated with poor second-order effects, while less promising initial impacts are the start of major chains.

Why do it that way?

The construction of a cross-impact matrix is the final stage in the representation of an organisation as a socio-technical system with economic purposes. All the previous stages are in their various ways essential preliminary steps in this direction. All the elements of the matrix – the variables themselves, the scores in the boxes, the potency and ease of change scores which may be used to weight the columns or to select row variables for special attention – are culled from the pooled experience of the members of the group which worked through the stages in the procedure. It represents their collective and agreed view of the nature of the connections between an all-inclusive list of dimensioned variables. Whether or not this collective view, that is, the matrix, represents accurately some reality out there beyond the assembled perceptions of the participants, can only be verified by acting upon the plan of change suggested by the analysis of the matrix and by recording the outcomes. It is possible for group members to learn much more about the organisation than hitherto if they do this, as we shall show in more detail in Chapter 4.

The first main reason for constructing the matrix is to identify the key variables on which to base a plan for changing the whole system in ways consistent with the objective chosen at the outset. The second is to provide a framework for subsequent 'learning by doing'. However, there are some important gains from the process itself as well as from the outcomes. To reach agreement about the number and the sign to be put into each box requires each member to dig deep into his experience and his capacity for logical thought and to be willing to defend the facts and logic on which his view of the matter is founded, or to abandon his opinions in the face of more and better facts, and more cogent arguments. It is an exercise in organisation logics which should leave not only a shared representation of the organisation but also a shared logic hammered out in the process of making the matrix, which includes all the partial logics but is greater than the sum of them. This is a large gain in terms of the efficiency of future communication between the members of the group, not to mention a shared vocabulary which supplements the professional and hierarchical ones.

It may sometimes happen that when all the knock-on effects through the matrix have been traced and key variables identified, the result corresponds to a previous insight claimed by one or more members. They may say that they would have reached the conclusion anyway without the time-consuming business of a group going through all the weary preliminaries and the construction the matrix itself . . . 'We've wasted all this time arriving at a conclusion known already'. There are two responses to this. To the individual(s) who makes the remark we answer that we now know the detailed factual and logical reasoning that makes up his intuitions and that this is well worth knowing. Further, others who did not previously share either his insights or the path to them now do so and this is a clear gain for everyone; not just the knowledge but also the sharing of it. Finally, it could just turn out that the insights, shared as they now are, will not survive the test of action, so it is as well to have on record how they were arrived at so that corrections may be made enhancing the learning for all concerned.

More likely, the results of the analysis of the matrix reveal surprises, and sometimes there is in a group a feeling that they are too surprising to 'make sense' to the knowledgeable and experienced group who put the matrix together and are difficult to accept. There is in this case only one course of action, namely to check the whole process out again, the items, the variables, the dimensions, crosses, the potency and ease of change scores, and the scores in the cross-impact matrix. It is important that the outcome in the form of a plan should indeed 'feel right'. To the extent that it does not so is the level of commitment to the plans based on it diminished.

Finally, each person who was concerned in the construction of the matrix will now have become familiar with a method of planning change which is based on an explicit theory of organisation. Both the theory and the method are transportable and will serve him/her well in other organisation settings in the future.

The difficulties

The construction of a cross-impact matrix demands mental stamina and social cooperation of an order not commonly encountered in the day-to-day life of organisation members.

To place an agreed score in every box of a large matrix needs not only mature and considered reflection by each group member on the nature of the relationships of cause and effect between two variables, but also the capacity to explain cogently his/her view of the matter and measure it against the views of others.

When confronted, as is likely, with a matrix with literally hundreds of boxes, and contemplating alternative uses of time, there is a strong temptation to try to hurry matters along. This can be done by deferring to those in the group who express strong views, who have long experience, or who claim special expertise, and suppressing one's own. It is not so difficult to pretend in justification that any benefit that might result would hardly be worth the prodigious effort required especially as the outcomes, at this stage, cannot be clearly seen. The potentialities for organisational learning and group integration offered by the construction and use of the matrix may be thought to be outweighed by the demands on the time and energy of group members. In our experience, groups are reluctant to spend what seems inordinate amounts of time on matrix construction. Success in persuasion hinges much on whether time will be made available. The decision about this is for top management to make. If time is made available the task is still one requiring staying power and dedication.

To reduce time and the demand for staying power it is possible to split up the group and divide the rows of the matrix between the sub-groups. The sub-groups having put in the scores in the rows assigned to each of them, the total matrix could be assembled for inspection and for questioning by the whole group. The whole group is unlikely to go through every box again but some members are likely to raise queries about particular boxes, where they are puzzled and need the score explained. This is not a very good substitute for the whole group being involved in the discussion surrounding every box, but it is certainly a possible short cut, as is the device of delegating the first attempts to fill in the matrix to one or two members, who could consult as necessary with others as they went along and present the completed matrix to the whole group for discussion and possible modification.

Neither of these alternatives (which have been tried in practice) is a really satisfactory substitute and the time saved would not be very great. We look now at Case study 6.

Case study 6   The benefits of shared understanding*

Sam was the senior foreman of the press shop which converted raw materials into batches of products used by the building industry, using simple presses. Each shift of thirty men had its own foreman. Sam attended during the day and was responsible for the total performance of the shop.

The press shop delivered its output to a warehouse which supplied builders' merchants usually by telephone order on short delivery times. The loading of the press shop was done by a production planner who worked to a forecast of 'call-off' prepared by the marketing and sales department in consultation with the warehouse manager.

The market was expanding and was very competitive. The marketing and sales manager and the warehouse manager were becoming frustrated with the apparent inability of the press shop to deliver to the warehouse what was required, that is, enough products of the right size and shape and of good quality and at the lowest possible cost. They were in no doubt that there was an adequate supply of raw material to hand and enough technical capacity in the press shop to cope easily with forecast growth in demand and changes in product 'mix'. For some reason the press shop, although usually able to deliver in quantity, seldom got the 'mix' right. It was not too difficult to arrive at the conclusion that the press shop was being badly managed and to point the finger at Sam. Sam's resentment made dialogue difficult.

It took a trusted outsider to bring Sam together with the marketing manager, the warehouse manager and the production planner, to take a fresh look and to find out what needed to be changed if Sam was to meet the forecast. In the discussions, as Sam described his difficulties in meeting the official product targets, many hitherto unconsidered and related items came to the surface for attention, among which were:

- Physical conditions in the press room

- The structure of the operator's pay packet, particularly overtime and bonus earnings

- The varying properties and quantity of the raw materials delivered to the press shop

---

*This case (both analysis and outcome) is reported in detail in WARMINGTON, A., LUPTON, T. and GRIBBIN, C., *Organisational Behaviour and Performance*, Macmillan, London 1977, pp. 85–116 and pp. 208–216

- The characteristics of the production schedule (length of runs and range of sizes)

- Operator discretion in work methods

- Downtime caused by breakdowns and batch changeover

- Balance between sequential operations

- Manning arrangements and size of press teams

- The ratio of experienced operators to new starters

(The reader might care to puzzle out the connections between these variables and between each of them and the malaise reported from the warehouse, bearing in mind that it was not easy to find replacements for operators who left the shop.)

As it turned out it was possible to find dimensions for the variables and a wealth of relevant measurements. This facilitated the construction of a model of the system which included the labour market, the product market, the supply of materials and the press shop. This model was used to determine what needed to be changed to get the system into balance and what obstacles lay in the path of the agents of change.

Summary

The end result of the process described in this chapter is a picture of an organisation, or part of it, as an open socio-technical system. The picture will have been drawn in such a way as to pick out those variables which look most likely to set off the chain reactions which will change the whole configuration of variables in ways conducive to the achievement of the objective. But the picture represented by the cross-impact matrix has another use which is to facilitate organisational learning. The next chapter describes, among other things, how this can be done.

4   Learning from experience

Those who have been involved in the steps of our procedure so far will be committed to act on an agreed plan aimed at an agreed objective in an agreed time. That may seem to be the end of the matter; and so it would be if everyone in the organisation unit which was to be affected by the plan had been involved in the procedure for making it. That is unlikely and it is also unlikely that all the levers for change will be accessible directly to those who made the plan. Even if that were the case it is still possible that because of factual errors, bias in judgement or less than total involvement by some or all of the participants in plan making, the plan could still be an imperfect vehicle for the achievement of the objective.

For example, suppose that a group has been assembled composed of the top ten managers of a large company drawn from HQ and the divisions and including heads of specialist departments such as finance and personnel. Suppose also that they set objectives for the growth and profitability of the whole company such as 'increase the return on assets employed by 50% in five years'. They then as individuals generate lists of items to be attended to if the objective is to be achieved; they compare and contrast the lists and each explains why he (she) has included such and such an item, and they arrive at an agreed list. Their next step, as we know, is to find dimensioned variables for the items and to place crosses and arrows on each dimension. After scoring each item for sensitivity and potency they then complete a cross-impact matrix from which they identify the key items, that is, those with the greatest knock-on effect. This is the basis of the plan for change. It is highly probable, and it is certainly our experience as facilitators of such processes, that there will be disagreements at every step (about the sensitivity and potency of dimensions for example) which will as often as not to resolved not by reaching consensus but by compromise, by the seduction of powerful arguments from powerful people or by deference to specialist opinion. It is also possible that information and opinion might be withheld for reasons of personal pique or professional antagonism or to settle old personal scores. To be sure, our procedure is designed to ensure that disagreements are brought into the open and frankly faced; and consensus arrived at if possible. Indeed, it is this very process, encouraged by the facilitator, which knits the group together around the objective and the process of making a plan. But it is as well to recognise that differences will remain which will be reflected in the match of plan and objective – the means and the ends – and in the level of commitment to implement the plan. This being so one can hardly expect that those who have not been involved at all in making the plan will know its *raison d'etre* and the group processes involved.

That is why those who are to be affected by the planned changes should themselves be involved in similar processes, related specially to their own part of the organisation rather than to the whole organisational unit. Otherwise the changes, whatever they are, will not go as smoothly as might be wished. There are two main practical ways to organise such involvement. The first more or less repeats the steps already described going down through various levels of the organisation. And the second, a weaker version, is 'telling and selling'. We describe the two approaches in turn.

Top-down bottom-up

In the first the original group (in this case the ten top managers) breaks up the overall objective into sub-objectives for each sub-unit of the organisation they manage. For example, the objective 'improve RoE by 50% in five years' could become, for a manufacturing sub-unit, 'reduce the unit cost of production by 20% over the same period'. For a sales and marketing sub-unit the objective might become a sales target matched to production capacity, and so on. The objectives proposed by the original group must now be discussed with those responsible for the sub-units to make sure that the sub-objectives are considered feasible by those who have to achieve them. It is possible at this stage that the sub-objectives may be revised. It is also possible but much less likely that in the discussions the original group will wish to consider revising the overall objective and going over some of the steps in the procedure again so that the plan is revised accordingly.

In each sub-unit groups will be formed to make plans to achieve their particular sub-objectives and they will follow exactly the same procedures as the original group followed, each emerging with a plan and a commitment to implement it. The advantages of this way of proceeding, that is, by testing the 'top-down' plan against the experience and intelligence of 'lower order' organisational participants, are that some of the errors of fact and biases of judgement in the original plan will be revealed and corrected and everyone will learn things about the organisation which they did not previously know. To carry this approach to its logical conclusion would mean that everyone at every level would be involved and in a large organisation it would require an expenditure of time and mental energy that would be more than senior managers might at first be ready to allow. It will then be necessary to judge whether the resources which would be used up in overcoming resistance to the implementation of the plan would be greater or less than those used up by gaining commitment. If it is judged that to overcome resistance would be easier then a weaker version of the top-down-bottom-up approach may be adopted.

Top-down tell and sell

In this version only the level down from the top will define sub-objectives and will follow our procedure for plan-making. After that it will be 'telling and selling'. By this we mean that the senior managers will announce that certain objectives have been set to which they (the senior managers) are committed. The reasons why the objectives have been chosen and the derivation of the plans to reach them are explained. This is the 'telling'. The selling takes the form of persuading those who are inclined to be sceptical about the rationale of the objective and plan and who lack trust in mangement's capability to implement successfully, that they have nothing to fear; that their own best interests will be served by accepting and following the plans, and that senior managers will competently steer through the changes. Although questions and discussions may be allowed, even encouraged, the plan is unlikely to be modified. This is essentially a top-down procedure and it carries the risk that implementation will be costly and protracted.

It will be apparent that we favour the first of these two approaches in general. Although it may well turn out that the second one may be judged more appropriate in settings where employees at all levels place great trust and confidence in top management and are ready also to defer to their superior knowledge, we still generally prefer the first for the reason that it allows a fresh role for the plan-making process, namely, to act as an integrative force and agent of culture change. It integrates across hierarchical levels and vertical divisions by engaging multi-functional, multi-level, multi-professional groups in the plan-making process. At the same time it encourages the development of new methods of problem identification, diagnosis and problem solving, as well as encouraging the more cooperative stances that help mediate the inevitable conflicts and disagreements which beset organisations with complex structures of specialisation. It also has potential as an integrator *via* its use as a vehicle for organisational learning. This aspect of the procedure has not been given much prominence in this present account and it is one that clients, in our experience, tend not to be much interested in. Although there are part explanations for the neglect, the realisation of the gain to be had will we hope become clear as we develop the following theme.

Organisational learning

An organisation cannot learn. The term organisational learning can only mean *firstly,* that each individual member of the organisation can learn more about what it is and how it functions as a socio-technical system with economic purposes and *secondly,* that the knowledge and understanding gained can be more widely shared by the organisation members. We have already pointed out that usually the experience from which organisational participants learn is limited, so that what they learn tends to be partial and to depend very much on the jobs they have, their professional training and frames of reference, their hierarchical level, the extent to which they are interested in further and wider learning, and so on.

The procedure for plan making that we have described and illustrated in this book is designed among other things to make up a total 'picture' of the organisation-in-environment from the partial 'pictures' of the participants; one which is greater than their sum and which can be generally accepted and worked with. That is why the generation of variety is encouraged as a first step. The procedure pools the detailed partial experiences and makes it possible for everyone who has been involved to reach a common understanding of the way the organisation and its parts function. The learning becomes much less partial and much less personally idiosyncratic.

The completed cross-impact matrix represents that common understanding. This does not necessarily mean that it is a faithful and accurate representation of the organisation as a socio-technical system for all the reasons we have explored. The matrix therefore presents an opportunity for shared learning because it has been used to arrive at a plan for change and to gain commitment to making the changes. Its accuracy and completeness can be tested by making the planned changes and recording the outcomes not only as they affect the objective but also as they influence the configurations of complex relationships between the dimensions. In short, shared learning can take place *as a result* of making the changes but only if the effects of the changes on the total organisation system are carefully traced and recorded.

Suppose, for example, that the group has judged that a particular dimension is highly potent and that to change it would be fairly easy (score 5/4, say). Suppose also that the completed cross-impact matrix shows that movements along the dimension are judged to be capable of powerful knock-on effects. Let us also posit a high degree of organisation commitment arrived at by the two processes as described already; commitment, that is, to the idea that movement along the dimension in the direction of the arrow has high priority in the plan. When the change is actually made it could well be that the judgements about potency and blockages are exactly confirmed by the outcomes; that is, a small movement along the dimension is in fact associated with a large impact on the objective, and few obstacles are encountered. And as the effects of the changes to other dimensions are traced the quality of the judgements recorded in the cross-impact analysis can also be checked. At the end of the time period of the plan the extent to which its implementation has achieved the objective can also be recorded. In short, the reasons for the relative success or failure of the plan can be systematically traced and the knowledge gained can be put to use in improving and extending shared understanding of the system dynamics of the organisation, and ensuring improved future planning.

It will be obvious also by now that every change that is made alters in some way the nature of the relationship between the system elements that have been characterised as items or variables in our procedure. Once changed, for example, a variable might lose much of its potency. To make changes in operator training with the objective of improving productivity might have potent initial effects as predicted but diminishing returns from further increments of change in the same direction can be expected. The variable of operator training could well move from the top right-hand quadrant of the potency/ease of change matrix to the bottom left-hand quadrant. Equally, once the planned changes have been made the pattern and strength of the knock-on effects will also change giving rise to a need to re-draw the cross-impact matrix, to represent the new relationships between the variables.

To add to the complexities, changes external to the organisational unit which were unforeseen when the plans were in the making may raise obstacles or create opportunities. The high likelihood of such happenings makes continuous monitoring necessary for the very good reason that revisions of the original representations of the system as expressed in the weighted cross-impact analysis will have to be made as and when they occur.

The procedural implications of what has been said seem clear. The plan-making team(s) must continue beyond plan-making with a changed role. It is not advisable to give the job to a single monitor/recorder. Although he or she will certainly learn more about the socio-technical system in environment, unless the results of his/her labours are shared then the opportunity for continuous *organisational* learning, as we have defined it, will be diminished.

We suggest, therefore, that a record be kept which makes it possible to display the revisions made to the weighted cross-impact matrix as a result of planned or unanticipated changes. These revisions may take many forms, such as:

1   The addition of new items/dimensions.

2   Revisions of the potency weightings.

3   Revisions of the scores and signs in the boxes of the cross-impact matrix.

4   Revisions to the pattern of knock-on effects.

5   Changing items into objectives as the need arises.

If continuous learning is to take place the team(s) will have to assemble at intervals of a few weeks to consider what revisions are necessary as a result of the data prepared by the monitor/recorders. As time goes on the displays will exhibit the way the system has changed and is planned to change giving all the information needed for continuous learning by the multi-functional teams.

Other benefits to be gained by following the procedure outlined are *first*, the planning process serves as a powerful organisational integrator and mechanism of conflict resolution. *Secondly,* it increases the confidence of those who make the planned changes that the outcomes will not merely be a matter for personal praise or blame, although there may be reasons for that, but rather become information to be fed back into the procedure for continuous organisational learning. *Thirdly,* the significance of hierarchy is diminished, for the reasons:

1   That superordinates become providers of information to and colleagues of the subordinates they work with in the planning/implementation process.

2   That action for improvement emerges from what Mary Parker Follett described as the 'law of the situation', rather than the edicts of bosses whose system 'pictures' are necessarily simple and partial.

3   That respect for bosses is based more on their open contribution to the development of knowledge of the 'law of the situation' than to their formal authority.

Finally, we would claim for the procedure that if it is properly done it utilises to a much greater extent than other planning systems the talents and experiences of organisation members, and in that and other ways contributes to culture change, that is, the ways things are done, the sharing of values and the confidence and trust that inhere in inter-personal and inter-role relationships with beneficial effects on personal motivation and organisation effectiveness.

5 Choosing objectives

There seems to be no obvious difficulty in choosing an objective aimed at organisation improvement. No manager would claim that his organisation or the part of it that he manages is without its problems. Everywhere, in every organisation performance is never thought of as being as good as it could or should be. There is always a gap between what is and what someone thinks ought to be; costs are too high, sales targets are not being reached, new products and processes are not being developed quickly enough, labour productivity is too low, delivery dates are not being met, labour turnover is too high, there is not enough talent around to fill top management vacancies, and so on. It would appear therefore that the assumption implicitly made in Chapter 1 that improvement objectives already exist holds good and all that is needed is to define them clearly and find quantities to express them such as '*How much* improvement should we aim at over *what period of time?*'.

However, it is perhaps not so straightforward. There are some possible difficulties and it is the purpose of this short note to draw them to the attention of those who intend to use our procedure.

The difficulties arise *first* because no objective is an end in itself but is always a means to some other end. To the manager of a manufacturing department a cost reduction objective might be considered an end in itself and a challenge to his professional skill. To the managing director the same objective might be seen as one *means* among others to keep

prices down, his objective being to win a greater share of
the market. Similarly to set and to reach a sales target may
be sufficient in itself for the sales manager but may be
regarded by the finance director as a means to the optimum
utilisation of expensive capacity. We noted this means-ends
effect in Chapter 4. What we recommended there was that
sub-objectives for lower organisation levels should be derived
from the plans made to achieve higher level objectives. We
showed also that the procedure could then be used to make
plans to reach the sub-objectives, by a 'cascading' process.
In that way the hierarchy of organisational authority and
the logical hierarchy of ends and means could be made
consistent.

The *second* difficulty arises because objective setting and
planning originate at all hierarchical levels in organisations,
and not only at the 'top'. It is possible therefore that objectives
set and pursued at lower levels will actually frustrate objectives set at higher levels. For example, a higher level target
of short-term growth in volume of sales could be frustrated
by delays occasioned by the successful pursuit of an objective
of high quality in manufacturing, or by a policy of engineering
maintenance based on lengthy plant shutdowns, or by the
industrial relations negotiators offering high earnings to avoid
industrial action and/or high bonuses to stimulate high output, all of which could drive up labour costs and prices,
with a possible negative effect on sales volume where the
market is competitive. When defining lower-level objectives
it is therefore prudent to check whether they are in fact consistent with such higher level objectives as already exist. If such
objectives do not exist or are not clearly enough defined,
then the opposite of the 'cascading' process is necessary. That
is, sub-objectives should be 'gathered-up' as it were and
related to higher level objectives. They can then be modified
if they work against performance improvement at higher
levels or indeed at any level. Alternatively, the higher level
objectives themselves may be re-formulated.

To follow this kind of iterative process is much more
demanding than 'cascading'. As Burns once observed (Burns,
1966) organisations are amplifiers of communication going
down and filters of communication going up. 'Cascading',

therefore, is relatively easy because power and authority and the responsibility for outcomes usually increase with hierarchical level. It is less easy for a subordinate to modify a higher level objective by rational argument from his own sub-objectives than it is for a superordinate to alter lower-level objectives. Yet it would not make much sense to continue to work in detail with objectives which are not consistent up and down organisational levels, wherever the inconsistency lies.

Against this line of reasoning it might be objected that subordinates should not define objectives for themselves and make their own plans to achieve them, but only accept sub-objectives that are 'cascaded' down. To try to implement such a policy would surely work against initiative and smother any urge to improve matters that may exist at lower levels. In addition the detailed knowledge and experience of lower-level participants is lost to objective-setters and planners at top levels. Yet such knowledge is a necessary, even vital, input to the process of objective-setting and planning with organisational improvement in mind. It is therefore sensible to tap that detailed 'expertise' by encouraging the setting of objectives at each level in the light of the difficulties known and directly experienced at that level, and by using our procedure to organise it in the process of developing plans and priorities and commitment to implement them. Always of course, with the proviso that the lower level objectives are tested for consistency with those originating at higher levels. This process of testing will itself alert higher level participants to the need to clarify *their* objectives and to include lower level objectives as variables in their own planning processes. There are some resemblances here to the procedures of Management by Objectives; but unlike MBO our procedure provides a framework to organise the experience of subordinates at every level in great detail and through group processes.

Another source of possible difficulty in the process of objective setting lies in the tendency for all organisations, and particularly those which are both large and complex, to create specialist departments, each with its own work to do; each bounded off from other departments which have different professional expertise and different work to do. A large multi-product manufacturing organisation for instance is likely to have several plants each located in different places, perhaps in different countries, and it will also have specialised departments for personnel, industrial relations, finance and accounting, sales and marketing, purchasing, management services and research and development. It is commonplace that in such organisations objectives and plans originating in one specialist department can in their implementation have unanticipated negative consequences for other specialist departments. These are the lateral effects which could compound the 'hierarchical' effects already discussed. The research literature is replete with examples of this, illustrating the process by which decisions taken in pursuit of objectives designed to improve an organisation's competitive position can, via a complex chain of consequences, cause difficulties for personnel specialists trying to keep the organisation manned at the level required to meet the production levels demanded by those objectives. Naturally such outcomes are seen as frustrating by those who set the objectives and are often interpreted as arising from lack of understanding, withdrawal of co-operation, or lack of general expertise in other specialist functions or at other levels. It is easy, but not very helpful after the event to say to the initiator of policy 'why didn't you think of that?', 'why didn't you foresee that your plans would start off chains of consequences that would in the end prevent you from achieving what you planned?'. It would obviously be helpful if such consequences could be foreseen so that any obstacles could be identified in time either to alter the plans to take account of them, or to take steps to remove the obstacles.

The procedure we have described in this book is well suited for the task of identifying the obstacles to be overcome. It would mean, however, if we continue to follow our illustration, that in developing a plan to achieve an improvement in sales, we would have to include in the planning group representatives of those specialist departments who could possibly be affected by a sales policy – certainly manufacturing and personnel, including training and industrial relations, probably accounts and purchasing, possibly management services. In this case our means-ends chains, wherever they originate, run across as well as up and down the organisation, and our procedure would act as a device to co-ordinate the specialist departments.

An actual example will serve to illustrate how easy it is for specialists to miss or to ignore some of the complex causes of organisational influences because of what one might describe as 'expert myopia'. Some years ago one of us was asked to meet the senior management team of a medium-sized manufacturing plant, which was part of one division of a large engineering firm. The team wished to explore the possibility of using the Lupton–Tanner method as a means to plan and to achieve productivity improvement. In a private conversation with the personnel manager before the meeting, he strongly expressed the view that the main cause of the relative decline in productivity was an inappropriate payment system. The personnel manager was convinced that the problem of productivity would be resolved as soon as a better payment system was introduced. In turn, he argued, this improvement would have a marked positive effect on the profit performance of the plant and that in turn would improve the profit performance of the company. Here we can see a means-end chain including (1) improved payment system *leads to,* (2) improved productivity *leads to,* (3) improved company performance, and this, as I was to discover later would, (4) strengthen the case for investment cash from the parent company. Going 'upstream', as it were, the personnel manager thought that the improvement in the payment system would be gained among other things by changing the way work standards were set.

However, at the meeting the next day it turned out after a long discussion of possible causes that the management team was not convinced that changing the payment system was the main pathway to improved productivity. To modify the design of the product to make manufacture easier was, they thought, a better route. It was thought that would not only improve productivity but would also, as a side effect, positively affect the pulling power of the incentive which in turn would contribute to even greater productivity, and by its effect on costs, enhance plant efficiency, etc.

Having briefly pointed to a few possible problems our advice is to make sure that wherever in an organisation an improvement objective is formulated and the process of planning to achieve it is getting started, those above the level immediately concerned, those below that level, and those who are likely to be affected by consequences occuring laterally, are involved in the process of clarifying and quantifying the objective. If possible they should be involved also in the process of evolving a plan using our method. In this way the logic of improvement can be matched with the structures and processes of organisation and management, and the detailed knowledge and experience of the organisation's personnel can be mobilised as contributions to the process of organisational integration.

The lengths to which this is carried will depend upon a judgement of the balance of the costs and the resources used, and the benefits to be gained from the early identification of possible consequences of actions taken.

Conclusion

This all leads back to where we began, that is with an objective to pursue, and affords an opportunity to summarise very briefly what has been written in preceding chapters. The systematic method for achieving change described in this book is logically very straightforward but in most other respects very complicated.

The logical structure of the method is simply to generate variety and to follow some rules for reducing it in ways which lead to practical plans for change and to their smooth implementation. The group processes of generating the ideas and experience which make the logic come alive and which, step by step, promote commitment to changes consistent with the objective, are the source of many of the complications that inevitably arise but, as the case examples show, these are usually seen in the end as having been well worthwhile.

Reference

BURNS, T. and STALKER, G. H., *The Management of Innovation,* Tavistock, London, 1966